SPEEDLINK

SPEEDLINK

A Comprehensive pictorial study of the rolling stock used on this service 1977–91

Volume 2: The Air-braked 'New' Batches

David Larkin

crecy.co.uk

© 2024 David Larkin

ISBN: 978 180035 3145

First published in 2024 by Crécy Publishing Ltd

All rights reserved. No part of this book may be reproduced or transmitted in any form or by any means electronic or mechanical, including photocopying, recording or by any information storage without permission from the Publisher in writing. All enquiries should be directed to the Publisher.

A CIP record for this book is available from the British Library.

Publisher's note: Every effort has been made to identify and correctly attribute photographic credits. Any error that may have occurred is entirely unintentional.

Printed in Malta by Gutenberg Press

Crécy Publishing Limited
1a Ringway Trading Estate
Shadowmoss Road
Manchester M22 5LH

www.crecy.co.uk

FRONT COVER TOP No. 460081, an SPA in flame red livery at Scunthorpe Yard, August 1980. *Author's photo ref. W8872/DL*

FRONT COVER BOTTOM BRA No. 967547, taken at New Cross Gate CCE depot on 15 September 1982, is loaded with new conductor rails and is in flame red/black livery. *Author's photo ref. W11903/DL*

BACK COVER MAIN No. 550000, taken at Trawsfynydd loading point in April 1971, is a Diagram 2/534 50T FLATROL MJJ wagon in original condition. It is in freight brown livery with white lettering and FLATROL MJJ code. *Author's photo ref. W3413/DL*

BACK COVER TOP No. 950340, taken at Hoo Junction Yard on 6 March 1983, is a Design Code BD006C BDA 80T steel carrier in original condition with a full complement of stanchions and loaded with narrow steel bars. It is in freight brown livery with white lettering and BDA code. *Author's photo ref. W12690/DL*

BACK COVER BOTTOM No. 360853, taken at Peak Forest on 23 February 1989, is an HBA hopper mineral wagon, resprung as an HEA. It is in Sector dark grey/yellow livery with white lettering, HEA code and RfD Sector symbol. *Author's photo ref. W15308/DL*

Contents

	Abbreviations	6
	Introduction	7
1	Liveries, Symbols and Lettering on BR-owned Stock	13
2	Design Code BB001 BBA 100T Bogie Steel Carrier	15
3	Design Code BD006 BDA 65T/80T Bogie Steel Carrier	32
4	Design Code BP004 BPA 58T Bogie Plate Wagon	59
5	Design Code BR006 BRA 49T Borail Wagon	64
6	Design Code FN003 FNA 50T Flatrol Nuclear Flask Wagon	70
7	Design Code HB001 HBA 46T Hopper Mineral Wagon	75
8	Design Code OB001 OBA 46T Open Goods Wagon	95
9	Design Code OC001 OCA 46T Open Goods Wagon	107
10	Design Code OD001 ODA 12T Pipe Wagon	115
11	Design Code SP020A SPA 46T Plate Wagon	117
12	Design Code VD001 VDA 40T Vanfit	125
13	Design Code VE001 VEA 12T Van [Ammunition]	137
14	Design Code VG001 VGA 24T Van [Sliding Wall]	144
15	Design Code XV005 XVA 80T Trestle Plate Wagon	147
16	Small prototype lots and air-piped conversions	150
	Conclusion	158
	Index	159

Abbreviations

AB	Air Braked
ABN	Air Braked Network
BOGIE STEEL AB	First code given to 100T Composite steel-carrying wagon
BSC	British Steel Corporation
C&W	Carriage and Wagon
CCE	Chief Civil Engineer
CFD	Central Freight Depot
CM&EE	Chief Mechanical & Electrical Engineer
COV AB	First code given to 45T Vanfit (full length doors)
COV CD	First code given to 45T Vanfit (centre doors)
DESIGN CODE	Post-TOPS identification of wagon design
DIAGRAM	Pre-TOPS identification of wagon design
FISHKND	Term indicating 'water' name of CCE wagons
GLW	Gross Laden Weight
MoD	Ministry of Defence
OPEN AB	First code given to 45T Open Goods wagon
PAD	Pre-Assembly depot for trackwork
PPW	Prawlia Polsowanij Wagonami (International wagon)
RAILFREIGHT	Name given to BR freight traffic
RfD	Railfreight Distribution Sector
RIV	Reglomento Internazionale Vagoni (International wagon)
SPEEDLINK	Term for 1977-1991 air-braked freight train network
STEEL AB	First code given to 45T steel-carrying wagon
TOPS	Total Operations Processing System
UIC	International Union of Railways

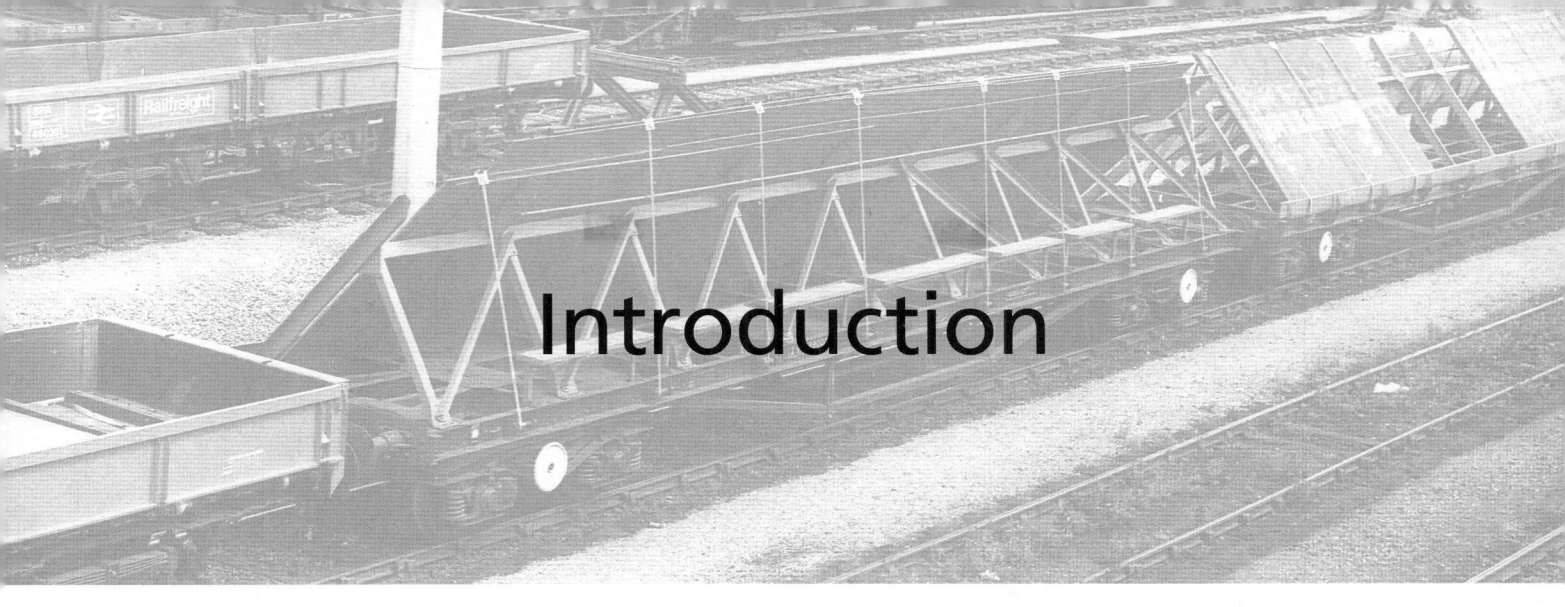

Introduction

By 1973, British Rail had taken delivery of sufficient air-braked stock to inaugurate fully air-braked trains, using the 100 OPEN AB (OAA) wagons and the 200 VAN AB (VAB) vans. The first such service was between Bristol and Glasgow, calling intermediately at Bescot and Warrington. Traffic conveyed included tobacco for Imperial Tobacco, chocolate for Cadbury-Schweppes, clay for English China Clay, soap powder for Proctor and Gamble, newsprint for Inland Distributors, drinks for Showerings, motor vehicles for British Leyland and aluminium for British Aluminium.

In addition to the OPEN ABs and COV ABs already mentioned, the vehicles used on the Western Region test train (see Volume 1, Chapter 5) were available, having been released to general traffic in 1972. Also available were the various ferry vehicles covered in Volume 1.

A further service was started in October 1973, running from Whitemoor yard (March) to Edinburgh and probably calling at Doncaster and Tyne yards.

ABOVE Brand-new VDA No. 200743 passing Latchmere Junction, Battersea, in June 1976 on a trip working destined for South Lambeth goods yard. *Author's photo ref. W6637/DL*

LEFT Brand-new OBA No. 110049, in company with three others, passing Factory Junction Signal Box with a Speedlink service from Dover, via Hoo Junction, Lewisham, Nunhead and Kensington Olympia, to Willesden (Brent) with vehicles which have arrived via the Dover train ferry in April 1977. *Author's photo ref. W7608/DL*

LEFT HBA No. 360040 is seen at Birkenhead Docks in new condition well loaded with industrial coal, probably for the Shotton Steelworks. This is one of the early wagons with central end ladder. *Author's photo ref. W8681/DL*

BELOW Brand-new BDA No. 950060, seen at Hoo Junction Yard in November 1977 with a full complement of stanchions. *Author's photo ref. W7538/DL*

The new network, probably at this stage referred to as the 'Air Braked Network' and carrying the black on yellow ABN disc symbol, grew rapidly and twenty-four services operated daily in 1976.

New air-braked types also began to be delivered, notably the OBA open wagon, seen on page 7, and the VDA van, seen on page 7. A government grant of £12 million was given for the construction of 500 OBAs and 300 VDAs.

The government grant mentioned earlier also included 200 BDA steel carriers, as seen in the photographs of 950060, but these were refurbished existing wagons of the BDO class dating from the 1950s.

BELOW BDA No. 950812, seen at Scunthorpe (Gunness) in August 1980, is in flame red livery with the double-arrow/Railfreight symbols. *Author's photo ref. W9112/DL*

Other new types to appear were the air-braked SPA plate wagon (see front cover), the larger version of the BOGIE STEEL AB (BAB), the BBA (see front cover) and the HBA domestic coal hopper (see page 8).

The standard 20ft 9in wheelbase on the newly-constructed four-wheeled opens and vans proved to be unsuitable for Ministry of Defence locations with tight curves and two types, the VEA, as illustrated by 230002, and the ODA (see page 10), were refurbished existing vehicles.

Other refurbishments of existing wagons catered for the more specialised needs of the steel industry, namely the XVA Trestle wagon, as illustrated by 99005, the BRA Borail wagon (see page 10) and the BPA bogie plate wagon (see page 11).

Brand-new XVA No. 990005, seen at Scunthorpe Yard in August 1980, is in flame red/black livery. A similar wagon is on the right and appears to have smaller plates as the load. *Author's photo ref. W8880/DL*

Further new types to appear were the OCA (see page 11) and the VGA (see page 10).

Finally, there were the air-braked nuclear flask wagons which were modified in later years according to Health & Safety regulations (see page 12).

These types, mentioned previously, formed the core of the British Rail-owned wagon fleet available for air-braked services.

There were a few experimental types which will be covered in the relevant chapters in this volume.

Brand-new VEA No. 230002, with another similar van, passing Longhedge Junction, Battersea, on a Speedlink service from Dover, via Ashford, Maidstone East, Swanley, Nunhead and Kensington Olympia, to Willesden (Brent). The van on the right is a ferry van from Europe which has arrived via the Dover train ferry. *Author's photo ref. W6884/DL*

ABOVE BRA No. 967547, taken at New Cross Gate CCE depot on 15 September 1982, is loaded with new conductor rails and is in flame red/black livery. *Author's photo ref. W11903/DL*

LEFT Brand-new VGA No. 210632, taken at Salisbury on 10 June 1983, is in unpainted/flame red/black livery with double-arrow/Railfreight and Speedlink symbols. *Author's photo ref. W13088/DL*

ODA No. 113017, taken at Severn Tunnel Junction on 19 November 1983, is in flame red/grey livery with double-arrow/Railfreight symbol. *Author's photo ref. W13526/DL*

Some building programmes were cut back according to traffic requirements and there were modifications to some designs, particularly to the type of springs used and the bogies.

In an attempt to bring CCE traffic within the remit of the air-braked fleet, there were many transfers of air-braked wagons to the CCE fleet, including all of the BRA fleet, seen on page 18, which became the YLA MULLET initially, with later changes to YMA or YQA PARR. The chief types involved were the OAA, OBA and OCA open wagons, the SPA plate wagons and the BDA steel carriers.

Brand-new OCA No. 112024 is seen in Rochester Goods Yard in the company of other air-braked stock which will form a trip working to Hoo Junction Yard for attachment to a Willesden Speedlink service. *Author's photo ref. W10419/DL*

Brand-new BPA No. 965069, seen at Tees Yard in May 1981, is in flame red/black livery. *Author's photo ref. W9120/DL*

FNA No. 550026, seen at Hither Green station on 2 July 1992, is destined for the Dungeness nuclear power station. The bodywork is buff with white lettering on black panels. *Author's photo ref. W17268/DL*

Total re-buildings for new traffics involved VCA and VDA vans (to runner wagons), OCA opens and VDA vans (to timber wagons) and various coil wagons using BBA, BPA and SPA steel carriers.

In general, the coal-carrying types were not involved during the Speedlink period. Two of the HBA hoppers had been built as MFA ferrous wagons with box bodies and some HBAs were later classified as HSA with bottom doors sealed for this traffic. Others were initially reclassified and then totally rebuilt as barrier wagons on the nuclear flask trains.

Apart from the VGA sliding wall type van, which was introduced in 1981, British Rail did not really introduce any new designs and certainly no new bogie vans.

BR appeared to expect firms to provide their own stock and UK Government Section 8 Grants were available under the 1974 Transport Act to fund building programmes. Modern vehicles for bulk powders, such as cement, China clay, grain and starch, were built. A downturn in the oil market saw few newer wagons but suitable early vehicles were upgraded.

The term Speedlink was first used for the air-braked network from September 1977. Motive power on Speedlink services changed little on the Southern Region at least, with the Class 33 diesels being replaced by slightly morepowerful Class 47s. Class 47s were also seen on other regions as well as Class 25s, Class 26s, Class 27s, Class 31s, Class 37s, Class 45s and Class 46s.

On lines with overhead electrification, Class 85s, Class 86s and Class 87s were used and, at the very end, Class 90s.

Despite British Rail's best efforts, the high hopes of the 1970s and the acquisition of new traffic flows, such as Butterley bricks in 1983, Plasmor breeze blocks in 1986 and the resurgence of timber traffic in 1987 after the 'Hurricane', established traffic flows disappeared. Kellogg's traffic went in 1984 and the loss of the Rowntree's chocolate in 1987 saw the closure of York Dringhouses Yard. Severn Tunnel Junction Yard was closed in October 1987 and all European traffic was handled at Dover after the closure of the Harwich train ferry in January 1987.

A review carried out in the mid-1980s resulted in the setting up of 'Sectors': Coal, Construction, Metals, Petroleum and Railfreight Distribution (RfD). With RfD handling Speedlink, automotive and chemical traffic.

Railfreight Coal established its own network for wagon traffic by March 1987 and Railfreight Metals had set up a similar network by 1989. Railfreight Construction, with cement, and Railfreight Petroleum, with gas oil to railway fuelling points, continued to travel on Speedlink services but dwindled.

RfD and Freightliner were merged in 1988 and service reductions ensued in the Dumfries, Westbury and West London areas, together with the withdrawal of Speedlink services from Millerhill and Tyne yards. Other alterations were carried out and the new Speedlink network was termed 'NETWORK 90'.

Despite these changes, a further review was carried out and it was ultimately decided by the British Railways Board on 6 December 1990 to close Speedlink down with effect from 8 September 1991.

In view of the changes in attitude towards global warming and other 'green' factors, this would not have happened at the time of writing some 30 years later, particularly with the opening of the Channel Tunnel three years after the end of the services and the proliferation of European lorries on British roads.

The next volumes in this series will deal with the European wagons seen on Speedlink services followed by the UK privately owned stock.

Liveries, Symbols and Lettering on BR-owned Stock

This subject was covered in depth in Chapter 1 of the first volume in this series but the following table gives the details of the vehicles covered in this volume:

BBA: Lot 3857 wagons (910001-910120), Lot 3872 wagons (910161-910365) and Lot 3871 wagons (910367-910491) were delivered in freight brown livery with black bogies and with BBA code in white and 'NOT TO BE LOOSE SHUNTED' lettering. No symbols were applied. Lot 3959 wagons (910492-910591) were delivered with flame red ends, black solebars and bogies, with BBA code in white and 'NOT TO BE LOOSE SHUNTED' lettering. No symbols were applied. The flame red/black livery was also applied to repainted wagons from the earlier Lots.

BDA: Lot 3907 wagons (950001-950200) and Lot 3925 wagons (950201-950800) were delivered in freight brown livery, including solebar, and black bogies and underframe with BDA code in white. No symbols were applied. Lot 3965 wagons (950801-950900) and Lot 3968 wagons (950901-951250) were delivered with flame red upper sides and black solebars, bogies and underframe with BDA code in white. No symbols were applied initially but repaints, including the earlier Lots, received double-arrow/Railfreight symbols.

Wagons transferred to the CCE were recoded YAA BRILL. When repainted, they received yellow upper sides and black solebars, bogies and underframe. The DC-prefixed number, YAA code and BRILL name were in black.

BPA: Lot 3985 wagons (965000-965059) and Lot 4011 wagons (965050-965079) were delivered with flame red sides and ends, black solebars, bogies and underframe and BPA code in white. No symbols were applied.

Wagons transferred to the CCE were recoded YNA. When repainted, they received yellow upper sides and black solebars, bogies and underframe. The DC-prefixed number and YAA code were in black.

BRA: Lot 4012 wagons (967500-967649) were delivered with flame red stanchions, unpainted bolsters, flame red sides and ends, black solebars and bogies and BRA code in white. No symbols were applied.

Wagons transferred to the CCE were recoded YLA MULLET. When repainted, they received yellow sides and ends and black solebars, bogies and underframe. The DC-prefixed number, YLA code and MULLET name were in black.

Wagons transferred to the CCE with bolsters removed were recoded YMA PARR. When repainted, they received yellow sides and ends and black solebars, bogies and underframe. The DC-prefixed number, YMA code and PARR name were in black.

FNA: Original livery for Lot 3886 wagons (550008-550014), Lot 3928 wagons (550015 and 550016), Lot 4004 wagons (550017 and 550019), Lot 4040/4057 wagons (550019 and 550020), Lot 4049 wagons (550021-550026) and Lot 4063 wagons (550027-550050) is uncertain. When modified, these were a buff coloured superstructure with a natural metal finish, black bogies and white sun shield. FNA code was white on a black panel as was other lettering. No symbols were applied.

HBA: Lot 3885 wagons (360001-361998) were delivered in freight brown livery, with black springs and HBA code in white. No symbols were initially applied but some vehicles later received the double-arrow/Railfreight symbols.

When being repainted, either as HBA with original springs or HEA with Brueninghaus springs, the sides and sloping ends and lower sides were flame red, the end support boxes were rail grey and the solebar and underframe were black. The number box and HBA or HEA code was on the lower left-hand side. Above this, in white, were the double-arrow/Railfreight symbols but these were applied in varying styles.

OBA: Lot 3909 wagons (110001-110500) and Lot 3930 wagons (110501-110800) were delivered in maroon livery overall, including springs but with unpainted interior. The number box and OBA code were on the left-hand upper side and the double-arrow/Railfreight symbols on the right hand upper side.

When repainted, after being fitted with Brueninghaus springs, the outer ends and top two planks were flame red and the lower side planks and lower side were grey (shade varied). Solebar and underframe were black. The number box and OBA code were on the left-hand lower side in white. The double-arrow/Railfreight symbols were sometimes applied but these varied in size and position.

Wagons transferred to the CCE were recoded ZDA BASS. When repainted, they received yellow upper sides and ends, grey lower sides and ends and black solebars and underframe. The DC-prefixed number and YLA code were in white and the BASS name in black, although this varied from wagon to wagon. Wagons transferred to S&T were repainted in flame red/yellow with KDC-prefixed numbers and SATLINK lettering.

OCA: Lot 4014 wagons (112000-112399) were delivered in flame red livery with black solebar, buffer beam and underframe. The number box and OCA code were on the left-hand side and the double-arrow/Railfreight symbols on the upper right-hand side, both in white.

Wagons transferred to the CCE were recoded ZDA BASS. When repainted, they received yellow upper sides, grey lower sides and ends and black solebars, buffer beams and underframe. The DC-prefixed number and ZDA code were in white and the BASS name in black, although this varied from wagon to wagon.

Wagons transferred to the CCE, and rebuilt with lower, fixed sides, were recoded ZCA SEAHORSE. When repainted, they received yellow upper sides and ends, grey lower sides and ends and black solebars, bogies and underframe. The DC-prefixed number and ZCA code were in white and the SEAHORSE name in black, although this varied from wagon to wagon.

ODA: Lot 4030 wagons (113000-113049) were delivered in flame red upper sides and ends, rail grey lower sides and black solebar and underframe. The number box and ODA code were on the lower side towards the centre in white and the double-arrow/Railfreight symbols were on the upper left-hand side.

SPA: Lot 3839 wagons (460002-460601) and Lot 3962 wagons (460602-461101) were delivered in flame red sides and ends, with black interior, solebar, buffer beams and underframe. The number box and SPA code were on the far left-hand side and the double-arrow/Railfreight symbols on the next panel to the right.

Wagons transferred to the CCE were recoded ZAA PIKE. When repainted, they received yellow upper sides, grey lower sides and ends and black solebars, buffer beams and underframe. The DC-prefixed number and ZAA code were in white and the PIKE name in black, although this varied from wagon to wagon.

Wagons transferred to the CCE, and with doors sealed closed, were recoded ZCA SEAHARE. When repainted, they received yellow upper sides, grey lower sides and ends and black solebars, buffer beams and underframe. The DC-prefixed number and ZCA code were in white and the SEAHARE name in black, although this varied from wagon to wagon.

VDA: Lot 3855 vans (200650-200979), Lot 3890 vans (200980-200999), Lot 3856 vans (201000-201099) and Lot 3908 vans (210100-210399) were delivered in maroon livery, including solebar and underframe. The number box and VDA code were on the lower sides towards the centre and the double-arrow/Railfreight symbols were on the upper left-hand side.

Repainted vans were flame red on the upper sides and ends, dark grey on the lower sides with white number box, VDA code and symbols as above.

VEA: Lot 3918 vans (230000-230049) were delivered in maroon livery sides and ends with black solebar and underframe. The number box and VEA code were on the lower left-hand door, the double-arrow symbol was on the upper left-hand side and the Railfreight symbol was on the upper left-hand door.
Lot 3982 vans (230050-230109), Lot 4017 vans (230110-230399) and Lot 4028 vans (230400-230549) were delivered in flame red livery upper sides and ends and dark grey lower sides and black solebar, buffer beams and underframe with white number box, VDA code and symbols as above.

VGA: Lot 4023 vans (210401-210650) were delivered with natural metal sides, flame red ends, black solebar, buffer beam and underframe. The number box and VGA code was in black on the lower left-hand side. A red metal nameplate with double-arrow/Railfreight symbols was on the upper left-hand side and a similar red nameplate with Speedlink was on the upper right-hand side.

XVA: Lot 3961 wagons (990001-990049) were delivered with flame red framework, solebar and buffer beam and black bogies. The number box and XVA code were on the solebar towards the centre.

Relatively few of the wagons and vans covered in this chapter received Sector livery after the mid-1980s and those that did will be covered in detail in the appropriate chapter.

Certain groups of vehicles were rebuilt to new configurations, involving a livery change, and these will also be dealt with subsequently.

2
Design Code BB001
BBA 100T Bogie Steel Carrier

Design Code BB001 100T Bogie Steel Carrier (Lot 3857)

910001 to 910120 – Built to Lot 3857 by Ashford Works, May 1975 to March 1976; Design Code: BB001C; Length over headstocks: 50ft 9in; Length between bogie centres: 30ft 5in; Bogies: FBT 6 (Y25C); 3ft 1½in diameter wheels; Air disc-Wheel hand brakes at wagon ends; Change-over lever; 1ft 8 ½in Oleo Pneumatic Buffers; Roller bearings; Screw couplings; TOPS Code: BBA; Usual lettering: 'NOT TO BE LOOSE SHUNTED'.

910121 to 910160 were issued under Lot 3871 but, for unexplained reasons, these wagons were built as 910367 to 910491 (qv).

No. 910042, taken at Ashford Works in October 1975, is a Design Code BB001C BBA bogie steel carrier. It is seen here in brand-new condition before the fitting of stanchions and in freight brown livery with BBA code. *Author's photo ref. W5111/DL*

No. 910073, taken at Warrington Dallam Goods Yard in March 1978, is a Design Code BB001C BBA bogie steel carrier. It is seen here in original condition with a full complement of stanchions and in freight brown livery with BBA code. *Author's photo ref. W8834/DL*

No. 910102, taken at Birkenhead Docks in February 1980, is a Design Code BB001C BBA bogie steel carrier. It is seen here in original condition but without stanchions and in freight brown livery with BBA code. *Author's photo ref. W8836/DL*

No. 910099, taken at BSC Shelton steelworks, Etruria, Stoke-on-Trent on 19 March 1983, is a Design Code BB001C BBA bogie steel carrier. It is seen here in original condition with stanchions and a steel billet load and in freight brown livery with BBA code. *Author's photo ref. W12928/DL*

ABOVE No. 910081, taken at Ebbw Vale Steelworks on 20 November 1983, is a Design Code BB001C BBA bogie steel carrier. It is seen here in original condition with a partial complement of stanchions and strip coil loaded 'eye-to-sky' and in freight brown livery with BBA code. *Author's photo ref. W13682/DL*

RIGHT No. 910080, taken at Warrington Dallam Goods Yard in November 1977, is a Design Code BB001C BBA bogie steel carrier. It is seen here in original condition with a full complement of stanchions and square section steel bars and in freight brown livery with BBA code. *Author's photo ref. W8835/DL*

RIGHT No. 910037, taken at Margam Yard on 12 March 1983, is a Design Code BB001C BBA bogie steel carrier. It is seen here in original condition with a partial complement of stanchions and strip coil loaded 'eye-to-sky' and in freight brown livery with BBA code. *Author's photo ref. W12795/DL*

ABOVE No. 910013, taken at Ebbw Vale Steelworks on 20 November 1983, is a Design Code BB001C BBA bogie steel carrier. It is seen here in original condition with a partial complement of stanchions and strip coil loaded 'eye-to-sky' and repainted in flame red/black livery with BBA code. *Author's photo ref. W13681/DL*

LEFT No. 910008, taken at Warrington Walton Old Junction Yard on 20 February 1982, is a Design Code BB001C BBA bogie steel carrier. It is seen here in original condition without stanchions and repainted in flame red/black livery with BBA code. *Author's photo ref. W10587/DL*

LEFT No. 910039, taken at BSC Shelton Steelworks, Etruria, Stoke-on-Trent, on 19 March 1983, is a Design Code BB001C BBA bogie steel carrier. It is seen here in original condition with a partial complement of stanchions and a load of steel billets and repainted in flame red/black livery with BBA code. *Author's photo ref. W12929/DL*

No. 910054, taken at Margam Yard on 12 March 1983, is a Design Code BB001C BBA bogie steel carrier. It is seen here in original condition with a partial complement of stanchions and strip coil loaded 'eye-to-sky' and repainted in flame red/black livery with BBA code. *Author's photo ref. W12784DL*

No. 910343, taken at Birkenhead Docks in February 1980, is a Design Code BB001B BBA bogie steel carrier. It is seen here in original condition without stanchions and in freight brown livery with BBA code. *Author's photo ref. W8837/DL*

Design Code BB001 100T Bogie Steel Carrier (Lot 3872)

910161 to 910365 – Built to Lot 3872 by Ashford Works, April 1977 to November 1977; Design Code: BB001B; Length over headstocks: 50ft 9in; Length between bogie centres: 30ft 5in; Bogies: FBT 6 (Y25C); 3ft 1½in diameter wheels; Air disc-Wheel hand brakes at wagon ends; 1ft 8½in Oleo Pneumatic Buffers; Roller bearings; Screw couplings; TOPS Code: BBA; Usual lettering: 'NOT TO BE LOOSE SHUNTED'.

910366 was part of the above Lot 3872 but was actually built as 920000 to Lot 3896 (see BLA entry in Chapter 16).

ABOVE No. 910335, taken at Ebbw Vale Steelworks on 20 November 1983, is a Design Code BB001B BBA bogie steel carrier. It is seen here in original condition with partial stanchions and loaded with 'eye-to-sky' strip coil and in freight brown livery with BBA code. *Author's photo ref. W13635/DL*

LEFT No. 910192, taken at BSC Shelton Steelworks, Etruria, Stoke-on-Trent, on 19 March 1983, is a Design Code BB001B BBA bogie steel carrier. It is seen here in original condition with a full complement of stanchions and steel billet load and in freight brown livery with BBA code. *Author's photo ref. W12927/DL*

LEFT No. 910323, taken at Mossend Yard on 26 October 1988, is a Design Code BB001B BBA bogie steel carrier. It is seen here in original condition without stanchion and recently repainted in flame red/black livery with BBA code. *Author's photo ref. W14251/DL*

No. 910344, taken at Mossend Yard on 26 October 1988, is a Design Code BB001B BBA bogie steel carrier. It is seen here in original condition without stanchions and loaded with 'eye-to-sky' strip coil and repainted in flame red/black livery with BBA code. *Author's photo ref. W14257/DL*

No. 910283, taken at Carlisle Citadel on 16 June 1992, is a Design Code BB001B BBA bogie steel carrier. It is seen here in original condition with partial stanchions and repainted in flame red/black livery with BBA code and double-arrow/Railfreight symbol on flame red panel. *Author's photo ref. W17185/DL*

No. 910309, taken at Carlisle Citadel on 16 June 1992, is a Design Code BB001B BBA bogie steel carrier. It is seen here in original condition with partial stanchions and repainted in flame red/black livery with BBA code and double-arrow/Railfreight symbol on flame red panel. *Author's photo ref. W17186/DL*

Design Code BB001 100T Bogie Steel Carrier (Lot 3871)

910367 to 910493 – Built to Lot 3871 by Ashford Works, November 1976 to April 1977; Design Code: BB001B; Length over headstocks: 50ft 9in; Length between bogie centres: 30ft 5in; Bogies: FBT 6 (Y25C); 3ft 1½in diameter wheels; Air disc-Wheel hand brakes at wagon ends; Change over device; 1ft 8½in Oleo Pneumatic Buffers; Roller bearings; Screw couplings; TOPS Code: BBA; Usual lettering: 'NOT TO BE LOOSE SHUNTED'.

A small number of this batch of wagons were converted for other traffics (see pages 30 and 31).

No. 910388, taken at Northwich Yard in February 1980, is a Design Code BB001B BBA bogie steel carrier. It is seen here in original condition with some stanchions and in freight brown livery with BBA code. *Author's photo ref. W10743/DL*

No. 910389, taken at Stoke-on-Trent Yard on 12 February 1983, is a Design Code BB001B BBA bogie steel carrier. It is seen here in original condition with a full complement of stanchions and in freight brown livery with BBA code. *Author's photo ref. W13110/DL*

No. 910404, taken at Warrington Walton Old Junction Yard on 3 October 1982, is a Design Code BB001B BBA bogie steel carrier. It is seen here in original condition with a full complement of stanchions and in freight brown livery with BBA code. *Author's photo ref. W12239/DL*

No. 910404, taken at York Dringhouses Yard in December 1978, is a Design Code BB001B BBA bogie steel carrier. It is seen here in original condition with a full complement of stanchions and a load of reinforcing rod and in freight brown livery with BBA code. *Author's photo ref. W8839/DL*

No. 910414, taken at Warrington Walton Old Junction Yard on 20 February 1982, is a Design Code BB001B BBA bogie steel carrier. It is seen here in original condition with some short stanchions and in freight brown livery with BBA code. *Author's photo ref. W10591/DL*

No. 910460, taken at Tees Yard in May 1981, is a Design Code BB001B BBA bogie steel carrier. It is seen here in original condition with a full complement of stanchions and in recently repainted flame red/black livery with BBA code. *Author's photo ref. W9094/DL*

No. 910378, taken at Mossend Yard on 14 February 1982, is a Design Code BB001B BBA bogie steel carrier. It is seen here in original condition with some short stanchions and strip coil loaded 'eye-to-sky' and in repainted flame red/black livery with BBA code. *Author's photo ref. W14260/DL*

No. 910458, taken at Ebbw Vale Steelworks on 20 November 1983, is a Design Code BB001B BBA bogie steel carrier. It is seen here in original condition without stanchions and strip coil loaded 'eye-to-sky' and in recently repainted flame red/black livery with BBA code. *Author's photo ref. W13680/DL*

No. 910479, taken at BSC Shelton Steelworks, Etruria, Stoke-on-Trent, on 19 March 1983, is a Design Code BB001B BBA bogie steel carrier. It is seen here in original condition with partial stanchions and in repainted flame red/black livery with BBA code. *Author's photo ref. W12933/DL*

No. 910498, taken at Portsmouth Fratton Goods Yard in December 1979, is a Design Code BB001B BBA bogie steel carrier. It is seen here in brand-new condition without stanchions and in flame red/black livery with BBA code. Author's photo ref. W8840A/DL

Design Code BB001 100T Bogie Steel Carrier (Lot 3959)

910492 to 910591 – Built to Lot 3959 by Ashford Works, December 1979 to October 1981; Design Code: BB001B; Length over headstocks: 50ft 9in; Length between bogie centres: 30ft 5in; Bogies: FBT 6 (Y25C); 3ft 1½in diameter wheels; Air disc-Wheel hand brakes on bogies; Change over device; 1ft 8½in Oleo Pneumatic Buffers; Roller bearings; Screw couplings; TOPS Code: BBA; Usual lettering: 'NOT TO BE LOOSE SHUNTED'.

910592 to 910691 were allocated to Lot 3959 but were never built. Vehicles delivered after 910545 had lifting points on the solebar above the bogies but the precise function of these fittings is not known. All vehicles were delivered in flame red/black livery.

No. 910498, taken at Margam Yard on 12 March 1983, is a Design Code BB001C BBA bogie steel carrier. It is seen here in original condition without stanchions and in flame red/black livery with BBA code. Author's photo ref. W12811DL

No. 910505, taken at Mossend Yard on 26 October 1988, is a Design Code BB001B BBA bogie steel carrier. It is seen here in original condition with some short stanchions and strip coil loaded 'eye-to-sky' and in flame red/black livery with BBA code. *Author's photo ref. W14259/DL*

No. 910521, taken at Ebbw Vale Steelworks, is a Design Code BB001B BBA bogie steel carrier. It is seen here in original condition with a full complement of stanchions and strip coil loaded 'eye-to-sky' and in flame red/black livery with BBA code. *Author's photo ref. W13670/DL*

No. 910535, taken at Warrington Walton Old Junction Yard, is a Design Code BB001B BBA bogie steel carrier. It is seen here in original condition with a full complement of stanchions and in flame red/black livery with BBA code. *Author's photo ref. W10586/DL*

No. 910562, taken at Llandeilo Junction yard in July 1981, is a Design Code BB001B BBA bogie steel carrier. It is seen here in original condition with a full complement of stanchions and in flame red/black livery with BBA code. *Author's photo ref. W10586/DL*

No. 910547, taken at Margam Yard on 16 April 1983, is a Design Code BB001B BBA bogie steel carrier. It is seen here in original condition without stanchions and in flame red/black livery with BBA code. *Author's photo ref. W12812/DL*

No. 910582, taken at Nunhead in September 1981, is a Design Code BB001B BBA bogie steel carrier. It is seen here in brand-new condition without stanchions and in flame red/black livery with BBA code. *Author's photo ref. W9096/DL*

No. 910588, taken at Hoo Junction Yard on 13 November 1982, is a Design Code BB001B BBA bogie steel carrier. It is seen here in original condition with partial stanchions and in flame red/black livery with BBA code. *Author's photo ref. W12427/DL*

Design Code BB001 100T Bogie Steel Carrier (Conversions)

BBA Coil Wagons (Design Code BB001D)

A significant number of BBAs were converted to carry strip coil in six lateral cradles with the ends removed, as illustrated by 910428. Known numbers were as follows:

910003/6; 910112/70/5; 910216/23/34/5/58/64/9/75/92; 910413/21-8/40/1/7/50/61/5/9/84/9

No. 910428, taken at Tees Yard in May 1981, is a Design Code BB001B BBA bogie steel carrier converted to carry strip coil as a Design Code BB001D. It is seen here in weathered flame red/black livery with freight brown cradles and retaining the BBA code. *Author's photo ref. wW9093/DL*

No. 910425, taken at Tees Yard in May 1981, is a Design Code BB001B BBA bogie steel carrier converted to carry strip coil. It is seen here in weathered freight brown livery with freight brown cradles and retaining the BBA code. *Author's photo ref. W9091/DL*

No. 910427, taken at Tees Yard in May 1981, is a Design Code BB001B BBA bogie steel carrier converted to carry strip coil. It is seen here in weathered flame red/black livery with freight brown cradles and retaining the BBA code. *Author's photo ref. W9092/DL*

These were allocated to Pool 2019 and conveyed steel slabs from BSC Tinsley Park, Sheffield, to BSC Lackenby, Middlesbrough, for conversion into hot rolled coil to be returned to Tinsley.

No. 910000, taken at Tinsley Yard, Sheffield, on 31 May 1992, is a Design Code BB001A BBA bogie steel carrier converted to carry hot metal slabs covered by a container with insulation. It is seen here in flame red/black livery with black container and BUA code and double-arrow/Railfreight symbol on a flame red panel. *Author's photo ref. W16997/DL*

BUA Wagons

910000, which was converted from the prototype BBA (built to Lot 3845 by Ashford Works in November 1973), carried hot metal slabs between various BSC steelworks, including Lackenby, Middlesbrough and Workington, and may have appeared before the demise of Speedlink.

Other BBA conversions, such as the BLA (910016, 910172/7, 910232/94, 910353, 910401 and 910573/88), the BRA (910163), the BWA (910234/6/69, 910413/21/2/6/40/50/84/9), the BXA (910465/9) and the round ingot wagons (910451/96) were all done after Speedlink.

3
Design Code BD006
BDA 65T/80T Bogie Steel Carrier

950000 – Ex-B942052; Converted to Lot 3888 by Swindon Works, October 1975; Design Code: BD006B; Length over headstocks: 52ft 0in; Length between bogie centres: 40ft 0in; Bogies: FBT 6 (Y25C); 3ft 1½in diameter wheels; Air block brakes on bogies and single hand lever; 1ft 8½in Oleo Pneumatic Buffers; Roller bearings; Screw couplings; TOPS Code: BDA; No lettering carried.

By 1983, this wagon had been transferred to the CM&EE department and was operating on the Southern Region (see page 33).

When originally converted from the original host wagons (either BDOs or JMVs), the original six bolsters were retained, including the option to move the outer pair to the wagon ends, but with a significant increase in the stanchion slots on each bolster. The chains were replaced by blue straps secured by ratchets on the solebar. Air brake pipework operated shoes on the Y25C bogies and hydraulic buffers were fitted. Early conversions retained a single hand brake lever per side but this was later changed to a disc on the bogie side.

No. 950000, taken at Scunthorpe (Gunness) in August 1980, is a Design Code BD006B BDA 80T steel carrier in original condition with some stanchions. It is in freight brown livery with white lettering and BDA code. *Author's photo ref. W9097/DL*

No. ADC950000, taken at Selhurst EMU Depot, Croydon, on 26 April 1983, is a Design Code BD006B BDA 80T steel carrier in original condition with some stanchions and transferred to the CM&EE. It is in freight brown livery with crude white lettering E, 38T MAX and YNA code. *Author's photo ref. W9097/DL*

Design Code BD006 80T GLW Bogie Steel Carrier Lot 3907 vehicles

950001 to 950200 – Converted to Lot 3907 by Ashford Works, October 1977 to August 1978; Design Code: BD006A; Length over headstocks: 52ft 0in; Length between bogie centres: 40ft 0in; Bogies: FBT 6 (Y25C); 3ft 1½in diameter wheels; Air block brakes on bogies and single hand lever; 1ft 8½in Oleo Pneumatic Buffers; Roller bearings; Screw couplings; TOPS Code: BDA; No lettering carried.

No. 950137, taken at Maidstone West Goods Yard in April 1978 as part of an exhibition train, is a Design Code BD006A BDA 80T steel carrier in brand-new condition with a full complement of stanchions. It is in freight brown livery with white lettering and BDA code. *Author's photo ref. W7547/DL*

No. 950014, taken at Factory Junction, Battersea, in October 1977, is a Design Code BD006A BDA 80T steel carrier in brand-new condition with a full complement of stanchions. It is in freight brown livery with white lettering and BDA code. *Author's photo ref. W7674/DL*

No. 950069, taken at Longhedge Junction, Battersea, in October 1977, is a Design Code BD006A BDA 80T steel carrier in brand-new condition with a full complement of stanchions and loaded with steel reinforcing rod. It is in freight brown livery with white lettering and BDA code. *Author's photo ref. W7344/DL*

ABOVE No. 950148, taken at Clay Cross in October 1978, is a Design Code BD006A BDA 80T steel carrier in original condition with a full complement of stanchions and loaded with short steel bars. It is in freight brown livery with white lettering and BDA code. *Author's photo ref. W7252/DL*

CENTRE LEFT No. 950078, taken at Burton-on-Trent Goods Yard in February 1979, is a Design Code BD006A BDA 80T steel carrier in original condition with a full complement of stanchions and loaded with steel bars. It is in freight brown livery with white lettering and BDA code. *Author's photo ref. W8843/DL*

LEFT No. 950140, taken at Tees Yard in May 1981, is a Design Code BD006A BDA 80T steel carrier in original condition with a full complement of stanchions. It is in recently repainted flame red/black livery with white lettering and BDA code. *Author's photo ref. W9102/DL*

Former identities of Lot 3907 vehicles: 950001 (B927022); 950002 (B942378); 950003 (B942468); 950004 (B942836); 950005 (B942324); 950006 (B927254); 950007 (B942857); 950008 (B942737); 950009 (B941857); 950010 (B942207); 950011 (B927399); 950012 (B927108); 950013 (B942630); 950014 (B927009); 950015 (B927075); 950016 (B941872); 950017 (B927270); 950018 (B942684); 950019 (B942568); 950020 (B942472); 950021 (B942382); 950022 (B942569); 950023 (B942187); 950024 (B942190); 950025 (B927007); 950026 (B941910); 950027 (B927211); 950028 (B942240); 950029 (B927364); 950030 (B942174); 950031 (B941966); 950032 (B927236); 950033 (B927318); 950034 (B927033); 950035 (B942893); 950036 (B942800); 950037 (B942498); 950038 (B942362); 950039 (B942214); 950040 (B942605); 950041 (B942801); 950042 (B942704); 950043 (B942374); 950044 (B942303); 950045 (B942491); 950046 (B942391); 950047 (B941891); 950048 (B942328); 950049 (B942360); 950050 (B927273); 950051 (B927306); 950052 (B927201); 950053 (B927202); 950054 (B927339); 950055 (B942031); 950056 (B942218); 950057 (B942488); 950058 (B942248); 950059 (B927134); 950060 (B942037); 950061 (B942485); 950062 (B927327); 950063 (B941917); 950064 (B942228); 950065 (B942669); 950066 (B941792); 950067 (B927206); 950068 (B942305); 950069 (B942466); 950070 (B942415); 950071 (B942912); 950072 (B942039); 950073 (B942314); 950074 (B927374); 950075 (B941468); 950076 (B942536); 950077 (B941685); 950078 (B942104); 950079 (B941593); 950080 (B927256); 950081 (B927396); 950082 (B942916); 950083 (B942648); 950084 (B927097); 950085 (B942878); 950086 (B941837); 950087 (B941768); 950088 (B941773); 950089 (B941481); 950090 (B927070); 950091 (B927109); 950092 (B941270); 950093 (B941273); 950094 (B927103); 950095 (B941347); 950096 (B941334); 950097 (B942096); 950098 (B942345); 950099 (B941847); 950100 (B942268); 950101 (B927299); 950102 (B942352); 950103 (B941832); 950104 (B942124); 950105 (B942261); 950106 (B942223); 950107 (B942808); 950108 (B942405); 950109 (B942301); 950110 (B942162); 950111 (B942389); 950112 (B942346); 950113 (B927127); 950114 (B941823); 950115 (B942653); 950116 (B942048); 950117 (B927349); 950118 (B942208); 950119 (B942182); 950120 (B942727); 950121 (B941893); 950122 (B927313); 950123 (B942829); 950124 (B942633); 950125 (B942363); 950126 (B942694); 950127 (B941888); 950128 (B942193); 950129 (B942103); 950130 (B942490); 950131 (B942580); 950132 (B942748); 950133 (B927398); 950134 (B942098); 950135 (B942806); 950136 (B927088); 950137 (B942171); 950138 (B942524); 950139 (B942449); 950140 (B942079); 950141 (B942707); 950142 (B942407); 950143 (B927379); 950144 (B927300); 950145 (B942279); 950146 (B942462); 950147 (B927371); 950148 (B927074); 950149 (B942390); 950150 (B942257); 950151 (B942428); 950152 (B927146); 950153 (B927332); 950154 (B942264); 950155 (B927086); 950156 (B941900); 950157 (B927121); 950158 (B942838); 950159 (B942394); 950160 (B942310); 950161 (B941820); 950162 (B941844); 950163 (B942722); 950164 (B942043); 950165 (B927378); 950166 (B942844); 950167 (B941809); 950168 (B942450); 950169 (B942304); 950170 (B927264); 950171 (B941904); 950172 (B942645); 950173 (B942657); 950174 (B942462); 950175 (B942544); 950176 (B942697); 950177 (B942090); 950178 (B942478); 950179 (B942381); 950180 (B942597); 950181 (B942054); 950182 (B942008); 950183 (B942888); 950184 (B942241); 950185 (B927356); 950186 (B941981); 950187 (B942688); 950188 (B942380); 950189 (B927167); 950190 (B942179); 950191 (B927063); 950192 (B942283); 950193 (B942533); 950194 (B927350); 950195 (B942295); 950196 (B927131); 950197 (B942035); 950198 (B927026); 950199 (B927224); 950200 (B942562)

All Lot 3907 wagons were transferred to the CCE as YAA BRILL vehicles, except 950124/56 which had been withdrawn, no doubt due to accident damage. However, at some point a large number of vehicles (51) were returned to revenue earning as BMA wagons (see pages 56/57), a few as BTA (see pages 58) and even a few as BDA.

Design Code BD006 80T GLW Bogie Steel Carrier Lot 3907 vehicles in CCE Use

No. DC950092, taken at Hoo Junction Yard on 7 December 1988, is a Design Code BD006A BDA 80T steel carrier in original condition with a full complement of stanchions and transferred to the CCE and carrying pointwork. It retains freight brown livery with white lettering, YAA code and BRILL name. *Author's photo ref. W14494/DL*

ABOVE No. DC950066, taken at Leyton CCE Yard, Stratford, on 19 February 1989, is a Design Code BD006A BDA 80T steel carrier in original condition with tall stanchions and transferred to the CCE and carrying new track panels and pointwork. It retains freight brown livery with white lettering, YAA code and BRILL name. *Author's photo ref. W15044/DL*

RIGHT No. DC950019, taken at Hoo Junction Yard on 20 September 1989, is a Design Code BD006A BDA 80T steel carrier in original condition with a full complement of stanchions and transferred to the CCE and carrying scrap rail. It is in unusual olive green livery with white lettering, YAA code and BRILL name. *Author's photo ref. W16503/DL*

RIGHT No. DC950112, taken at Hoo Junction Yard on 7 December 1988, is a Design Code BD006A BDA 80T steel carrier in original condition with a full complement of stanchions and transferred to the CCE and carrying pointwork. It is in yellow/black livery with black lettering, YAA code and BRILL name. *Author's photo ref. W14493/DL*

Design Code BD006 80T GLW Bogie Steel Carrier Lot 3925 vehicles

950201 to 950800 – Converted to Lot 3925 by Shildon Works, August 1978 to September 1979; Design Code: BD006C; Length over headstocks: 52ft 0in; Length between bogie centres: 40ft 0in; Bogies: FBT 6 (Y25C); 3ft 1½in diameter wheels; Air block brakes on bogies and single hand lever; 1ft 8½in Oleo Pneumatic Buffers; Roller bearings; Screw couplings; TOPS Code: BDA; No lettering carried.

This batch, apart from the last few wagons, was delivered in the freight brown livery.

No. 950228, taken at Shepherds Lane, Brixton in April 1979, is a Design Code BD006C BDA 80T steel carrier in original condition with some stanchions. It is in freight brown livery with white lettering and BDA code. *Author's photo ref. W8847/DL*

No. 950793, taken at Warrington Dallam Goods Yard on 23 October 1988, is a Design Code BD006C BDA 80T steel carrier in original condition with a full complement of stanchions and loaded with steel H-girders. It is in new flame red/black livery with white lettering and BDA code and double-arrow/Railfreight symbol. *Author's photo ref. W14127/DL*

No. 950243, taken at Southampton Bevois Park goods yard on 1 February 1989, is a Design Code BD006C BDA 80T steel carrier in original condition with a full complement of stanchions and loaded with steel H reinforcing rod. It is in freight brown livery with white lettering and BDA code. *Author's photo ref. W14920/DL*

No. 950254, taken at Sheffield steel terminal on 22 October 1988, is a Design Code BD006C BDA 80T steel carrier in original condition with a full complement of stanchions and loaded with steel reinforcing rod. It is in freight brown livery with white lettering and BDA code. *Author's photo ref. W14099/DL*

No. 950286, taken at Hoo Junction Yard on 19 January 1989, is a Design Code BD006C BDA 80T steel carrier in original condition with a full complement of stanchions and loaded with steel U-channel. It is in freight brown livery with white lettering and BDA code. *Author's photo ref. W14838/DL*

No. 950309, taken at Burton-upon-Trent goods yard in February 1979, is a Design Code BD006C BDA 80T steel carrier in original condition with a full complement of stanchions and loaded with steel bars. It is in freight brown livery with white lettering and BDA code. *Author's photo ref. W8851/DL*

No. 950460, taken at Ridham Dock, Sittingbourne, on 5 May 1984, is a Design Code BD006C BDA 80T steel carrier in original condition with a full complement of stanchions and loaded with steel reinforcing rod . It is in freight brown livery with white lettering an d BDA code. *Author's photo ref. W13658/DL*

No. 950589, taken at Hoo Junction Yard on 5 May 1984, is a Design Code BD006C BDA 80T steel carrier in original condition with a full complement of stanchions and loaded with steel U-channel. It is in freight brown livery with white lettering and BDA code. *Author's photo ref. W14527/DL*

No. 950362, taken at Nunhead in October 1981, is a Design Code BD006C BDA 80T steel carrier in original condition with a full complement of stanchions and loaded with steel H-girders with runners both ends. It is in freight brown livery with white lettering and BDA code. *Author's photo ref. W9104/DL*

No. 950454, taken at South Lambeth goods yard, Battersea, in April 1980, is a Design Code BD006C BDA 80T steel carrier in original condition with a full complement of stanchions and loaded with unidentified sheeted load. It is in freight brown livery with white lettering and BDA code. *Author's photo ref. W8859/DL*

No. 950340, taken at Hoo Junction Yard on 6 March 1983, is a Design Code BD006C BDA 80T steel carrier in original condition with a full complement of stanchions and loaded with narrow steel bars. It is in freight brown livery with white lettering and BDA code. *Author's photo ref. W12690/DL*

No. 950779, taken at Sheerness Steelworks on 5 May 1984, is a Design Code BD006C BDA 80T steel carrier in original condition with a full complement of stanchions and loaded with steel bars. It is in freight brown livery with white lettering and BDA code. *Author's photo ref. W13881/DL*

No. 950703, taken at South Bank sidings, Middlesbrough, in September 1981, is a Design Code BD006C BDA 80T steel carrier in original condition with a full complement of stanchions and loaded with steel H-girders. It is marshalled with RRV runners and not eligible for Speedlink services. It is in freight brown livery with white lettering and BDA code. *Author's photo ref. W9107/DL*

No. 950228, taken at Warrington Dallam goods yard on 23 October 1988, is a Design Code BD006C BDA 80T steel carrier in original condition with a full complement of stanchions and loaded with steel H-girders. It is in repainted flame red/black livery with white lettering, BDA code and double-arrow/Railfreight symbol. *Author's photo ref. W14133/DL*

No. 950606, taken at Ripple Lane Yard, Barking, on 1 May 1982, is a Design Code BD006C BDA 80T steel carrier in original condition with a full complement of stanchions and loaded with scrap rails. It is in freight brown livery with white lettering and BDA code. *Author's photo ref. W6283/DL*

Former identities of Lot 3925 vehicles: 950201 (B942636); 950202 (B942097); 950203 (B942191); 950204 (B927052); 950205 (B942847); 950206 (B942811); 950207 (B942406); 950208 (B942167); 950209 (B942662); 950210 (B942315); 950211 (B942064); 950212 (B942859); 950213 (B927119); 950214 (B942677); 950215 (B942780); 950216 (B927008); 950217 (B942262); 950218 (B942790); 950219 (B942621); 950220 (B942708); 950221 (B942158); 950222 (B942117); 950223 (B927229); 950224 (B927161); 950225 (B941927); 950226 (B942327); 950227 (B927151); 950228 (B942275); 950229 (B927823); 950230 (B927315); 950231 (B942114); 950232 (B942805); 950233 (B942049); 950234 (B927012); 950235 (B941852); 950236 (B942044); 950237 (B942709); 950238 (B942622); 950239 (B942448); 950240 (B942638); 950241 (B942300); 950242 (B941873); 950243 (B927269); 950244 (B942725); 950245 (B941830); 950246 (B942512); 950247 (B942564); 950248 (B942540); 950249 (B942541); 950250 (B942196); 950251 (B942687); 950252 (B942293); 950253 (B927359); 950254 (B942134); 950255 (B927277); 950256 (B942482); 950257 (B942070); 950258 (B927291); 950259 (B927248); 950260 (B942080); 950261 (B942458); 950262 (B942885); 950263 (B941870); 950264 (B942152); 950265 (B941892); 950266 (B941810); 950267 (B942486); 950268 (B942693); 950269 (B942092); 950270 (B927225); 950271 (B941957); 950272 (B927235); 950273 (B942095); 950274 (B942239); 950275 (B927343); 950276 (B942864); 950277 (B942706); 950278 (B942199); 950279 (B927233); 950280 (B941856); 950281 (B927381); 950282 (B942147); 950283 (B927197); 950284 (B941878); 950285 (B927154); 950286 (B942479); 950287 (B942288); 950288 (B942467); 950289 (B927020); 950290 (B927089); 950291 (B942520); 950292 (B941987); 950293 (B942230); 950294 (B941840); 950295 (B942623); 950296 (B927093); 950297 (B942331); 950298 (B941892); 950299 (B942423); 950300 (B927036); 950301 (B927122); 950302 (B942504); 950303 (B941899); 950304 (B941895); 950305 (B927325); 950306 (B942703); 950307 (B927129); 950308 (B942534); 950309 (B942444); 950310 (B942012); 950311 (B942089); 950312 (B942067); 950313 (B941941); 950314 (B942254); 950315 (B941859); 950316 (B942826); 950317 (B942237); 950318 (B942122); 950319 (B942866); 950320 (B927187); 950321 (B942084); 950322 (B942521); 950323 (B927072); 950324 (B942582); 950325 (B942173); 950326 (B942728); 950327 (B942699); 950328 (B942186); 950329 (B942131); 950330 (B942758); 950331 (B927276); 950332 (B941985); 950333 (B942760); 950334 (B942925); 950335 (B942555); 950336 (B927230); 950337 (B941921); 950338 (B927111); 950339 (B941849); 950340 (B927050); 950341 (B927114); 950342 (B942270); 950343 (B942086); 950344 (B942150); 950345 (B942827); 950346 (B942252); 950347 (B942149); 950348 (B942225); 950349 (B942839); 950350 (B927305); 950351 (B942416); 950352 (B942688); 950353 (B942563); 950354 (B942559); 950355 (B927294); 950356 (B942682); 950357 (B942535); 950358 (B927163); 950359 (B941980); 950360 (B927214); 950361 (B942663); 950362 (B942731); 950363 (B942537); 950364 (B927319); 950365 (B941884); 950366 (B942764); 950367 (B942587); 950368 (B942628); 950369 (B927027); 950370 (B942579); 950371 (B941802); 950372 (B942770); 950373 (B942713); 950374 (B941918); 950375 (B927191); 950376 (B942014); 950377 (B927344); 950378 (B942730); 950379 (B927160); 950380 (B941815); 950381 (B942278); 950382 (B941998); 950383 (B941974); 950384 (B942515); 950385 (B942159); 950386 (B942435); 950387 (B927094); 950388 (B942797); 950389 (B927005); 950390 (B927040); 950391 (B941869); 950392 (B927227); 950393 (B942365); 950394 (B942335); 950395 (B927176); 950396 (B927085); 950397 (B942245); 950398 (B927087); 950399 (B941874); 950400 (B927034); 950401 (B942339); 950402 (B942000); 950403 (B927241); 950404 (B942181); 950405 (B927278); 950406 (B942591); 950407 (B942003); 950408 (B942771); 950409 (B942584); 950410 (B927140); 950411 (B941923); 950412 (B942798); 950413 (B942457); 950414 (B927016); 950415 (B942796); 950416 (B941803); 950417 (B942776); 950418 (B927363); 950419 (B942666); 950420 (B942105); 950421 (B942712); 950422 (B941950); 950423 (B942502); 950424 (B942471); 950425 (B927346); 950426 (B942726); 950427 (B927001); 950428 (B941898); 950429 (B927360); 950430 (B942036); 950431 (B927263); 950432 (B941909); 950433 (B942019); 950434 (B927393); 950435 (B942865); 950436 (B941908); 950437 (B927053); 950438 (B927358); 950439 (B942690); 950440 (B941846); 950441 (B941951); 950442 (B941814); 950443 (B942921); 950444 (B942138); 950445 (B942123); 950446 (B941871); 950447 (B942125); 950448 (B941824); 950449 (B942399); 950450 (B941942); 950451 (B942729); 950452 (B942316); 950453 (B942379); 950454 (B942132); 950455 (B942256); 950456 (B927297); 950457 (B942673); 950458 (B942778); 950459 (B927334); 950460 (B942747); 950461 (B927325); 950462 (B942130); 950463 (B942715); 950464 (B942337); 950465 (B941901); 950466 (B927209); 950467 (B941867); 950468 (B941971); 950469 (B942480); 950470 (B927098); 950471 (B942822); 950472 (B942670); 950473 (B927348); 950474 (B942592); 950475 (B942470); 950476 (B927013); 950477 (B942410); 950478 (B942738); 950479 (B942753); 950480 (B942489); 950481 (B942759); 950482 (B927252); 950483 (B942006); 950484 (B927158); 950485 (B942746); 950486 (B942204); 950487 (B927076); 950488 (B941866); 950489 (B927035); 950490 (B942322); 950491 (B941799); 950492 (B942026); 950493 (B942869); 950494 (B942739); 950495 (B942711); 950496 (B942750); 950497 (B941875); 950498 (B942111); 950499 (B942859); 950500 (B942763); 950501 (B942119); 950502 (B942113); 950503 (B927253); 950504 (B942263); 950505 (B927107); 950506 (B942126); 950507 (B941979); 950508 (B942194); 950509 (B941947); 950510 (B927138); 950511 (B942917); 950512 (B942631); 950513 (B942027); 950514 (B942483); 950515 (B927266); 950516 (B927311); 950517 (B927042); 950518 (B941887); 950519 (B942112); 950520 (B942754); 950521 (B942626); 950522 (B927295); 950523 (B942081); 950524 (B941817); 950525 (B942754); 950526 (B942736); 950527 (B942461); 950528 (B942007); 950529 (B942678); 950530 (B942414); 950531 (B942177); 950532 (B942583); 950533 (B942813); 950534 (B942756); 950535 (B942755); 950536 (B942116); 950537 (B941978); 950538 (B927204); 950539 (B927375); 950540

(B941052); 950541 (B927316); 950542 (B942357); 950543 (B941894); 950544 (B927106); 950545 (B942141); 950546 (B927387); 950547 (B942588); 950548 (B941931); 950549 (B927044); 950550 (B927047); 950551 (B942413); 950552 (B942586); 950553 (B942355); 950554 (B927080); 950555 (B941819); 950556 (B942409); 950557 (B942209); 950558 (B942393); 950559 (B942762); 950560 (B942576); 950561 (B942010); 950562 (B927288); 950563 (B942271); 950564 (B942001); 950565 (B942040); 950566 (B942618); 950567 (B942522); 950568 (B942500); 950569 (B942773); 950570 (B942572); 950571 (B941955); 950572 (B942253); 950573 (B942484); 950574 (B927133); 950575 (B942343); 950576 (B942120); 950577 (B941925); 950578 (B927188); 950579 (B942418); 950580 (B941938); 950581 (B942285); 950582 (B942333); 950583 (B927128); 950584 (B942474); 950585 (B942635); 950586 (B942045); 950587 (B927135); 950588 (B942914); 950589 (B927368); 950590 (B942487); 950591 (B927361); 950592 (B942907); 950593 (B942266); 950594 (B942610); 950595 (B942632); 950596 (B942506); 950597 (B942206); 950598 (B942889); 950599 (B942765); 950600 (B942871); 950601 (B941890); 950602 (B942280); 950603 (B942659); 950604 (B942575); 950605 (B942629); 950606 (B942108); 950607 (B942176); 950608 (B941939); 950609 (B942153); 950610 (B941961); 950611 (B942574); 950612 (B941964); 950613 (B942787); 950614 (B927528); 950615 (B942412); 950616 (B942136); 950617 (B942258); 950618 (B942160); 950619 (B942928); 950620 (B942802); 950621 (B942494); 950622 (B927370); 950623 (B942627); 950624 (B942372); 950625 (B942029); 950626 (B927010); 950627 (B942761); 950628 (B927004); 950629 (B927279); 950630 (B927175); 950631 (B927116); 950632 (B927112); 950633 (B941911); 950634 (B942198); 950635 (B942018); 950636 (B942074); 950637 (B942668); 950638 (B942072); 950639 (B927139); 950640 (B927065); 950641 (B942720); 950642 (B942929); 950643 (B942881); 950644 (B941991); 950645 (B942902); 950646 (B942856); 950647 (B942918); 950648 (B941877); 950649 (B942860); 950650 (B942898); 950651 (B942154); 950652 (B941806); 950653 (B927304); 950654 (B942236); 950655 (B941818); 950656 (B942561); 950657 (B942224); 950658 (B942741); 950659 (B942189); 950660 (B927032); 950661 (B941881); 950662 (B941969); 950663 (B942816); 950664 (B942050); 950665 (B942552); 950666 (B942374); 950667 (B942812); 950668 (B942513); 950669 (B927240); 950670 (B942038); 950671 (B942102); 950672 (B942601); 950673 (B942853); 950674 (B942548); 950675 (B942483); 950676 (B942421); 950677 (B942338); 950678 (B942434); 950679 (B941889); 950680 (B941850); 950681 (B941963); 950682 (B941915); 950683 (B942069); 950684 (B927045); 950685 (B927112); 950686 (B942654); 950687 (B941913); 950688 (B927296); 950689 (B942887); 950690 (B927338); 950691 (B942057); 950692 (B942145); 950693 (B942923); 950694 (B927366); 950695 (B942139); 950696 (B942847); 950697 (B927054); 950698 (B942246); 950699 (B927255); 950700 (B942021); 950701 (B942503); 950702 (B942071); 950703 (B942767); 950704 (B942818); 950705 (B942292); 950706 (B941914); 950707 (B942595); 950708 (B941788); 950709 (B941880); 950710 (B942530); 950711

No. 950800, taken at Hoo Junction Yard in March 1981, is a Design Code BD006C BDA 80T steel carrier in original condition with a full complement of stanchions. It is in flame red/black livery with white lettering and BDA code and was one of the very few Lot 3925 wagons delivered in this livery. *Author's photo ref. W9109B/DL*

(B942259); 950712 (B942903); 950713 (B942908); 950714 (B942714); 950715 (B941886); 950716 (B941876); 950717 (B942637); 950718 (B942742); 950719 (B927335); 950720 (B927317); 950721 (B941893); 950722 (B927079); 950723 (B942613); 950724 (B927166); 950725 (B942128); 950726 (B942900); 950727 (B942553); 950728 (B941960); 950729 (B927231); 950730 (B941865); 950731 (B941831); 950732 (B942599); 950733 (B942387); 950734 (B942465); 950735 (B942340); 950736 (B942922); 950737 (B942155); 950738 (B942825); 950739 (B941959); 950740 (B927029); 950741 (B942681); 950742 (B942600); 950743 (B942824); 950744 (B927051); 950745 (B942088); 950746 (B942493); 950747 (B942311); 950748 (B942567); 950749 (B941812); 950750 (B927307); 950751 (B942845); 950752 (B927324); 950753 (B942024); 950754 (B927121); 950755 (B942701); 950756 (B942689); 950757 (B942400); 950758 (B927347); 950759 (B941992); 950760 (B942201); 950761 (B927123); 950762 (B942768); 950763 (B942615); 950764 (B927289); 950765 (B941943); 950766 (B942408); 950767 (B942312); 950768 (B942330); 950769 (B927002); 950770 (B942617); 950771 (B942475); 950772 (B942358); 950773 (B941790); 950774 (B942364); 950775 (B942794); 950776 (B942211); 950777 (B927281); 950778 (B942614); 950779 (B942894); 950780 (B927136); 950781 (B942419); 950782 (B927267); 950783 (B942251); 950784 (B927147); 950785 (B941797); 950786 (B927183); 950787 (B927246);, 950788 (B942133); 950789 (B927024); 950790 (B927194); 950791 (B927156); 950792 (B942499); 950793 (B927385); 950794 (B942183); 950795 (B927025); 950796 (B941794); 950797 (B927249); 950798 (B927184); 950799 (B942880); 950800 (B942876)

950564 and 950565 were fitted with a different bogie pattern but it is not known if others were similarly fitted (see page 46). Only 950201 and 950202 were transferred to the CCE to become YAA BRILL. There were a number of conversions to other types, viz BFA and BMA, as recorded on pages 54/55 and 56/57 respectively for details.

ABOVE No. 950612, taken at Hamworthy, Poole, on 13 March 1989, is a Design Code BD006C BDA 80T steel carrier in original condition with a partial complement of stanchions. It is repainted in flame red/black livery with white lettering and BDA code. *Author's photo ref. W15814/DL*

CENTRE RIGHT No. 950798, taken at Ridham Dock, Sittingbourne, on 5 May 1984, is a Design Code BD006C BDA 80T steel carrier in original condition with a full complement of stanchions and loaded with steel reinforcing rod. It is in flame red/black livery with white lettering and BDA code and was one of the very few Lot 3925 wagons delivered in this livery. *Author's photo ref. W13657/DL*

RIGHT No. 950565, taken at Scunthorpe (Gunness), is a Design Code BD006C BDA 80T steel carrier with unusual bogies in original condition, with a full complement of stanchions. It is in freight brown livery with white lettering and BDA code. *Author's photo ref. W9105/DL*

No. 950802, taken at Tyne Yard in September 1979, is a Design Code BD006D BDA 80T steel carrier in brand-new condition with a full complement of stanchions. It is in flame red/black livery with white lettering and BDA code. *Author's photo ref. W9110/DL*

Design Code BD006 80T GLW Bogie Steel Carrier Lot 3965 and Lot 3968 vehicles

950801 to 950900 – Converted to Lot 3965 by Shildon Works, September 1979 to December 1979.

950901 to 951250 – Converted to Lot 3968 by Shildon Works, March 1980 to March 1981; Design Code: BD006D; Length over headstocks: 52ft 0in; Length between bogie centres: 40ft 0in; Bogies: FBT 6 (Y25C); 3ft 1½in diameter wheels; Air block brakes on bogies and disc hand-wheel on both bogies; 1ft 8½in Oleo Pneumatic Buffers; Roller bearings; Screw couplings; TOPS Code: BDA; No lettering carried.

This batch dispensed with the single hand brake lever per side and had solid disc hand-wheels on each bogie. All were delivered in flame red/black livery.

No. 950806, taken at Scunthorpe Yard in August 1980, is a Design Code BD006D BDA 80T steel carrier in original condition with a full complement of stanchions and loaded with steel U-section girders. It is in flame red/black livery with white lettering and BDA code. *Author's photo ref. W8866/DL*

No. 950811, taken at Rochester goods yard in June 1981, is a Design Code BD006D BDA 80T steel carrier in original condition with a full complement of stanchions and loaded with steel H-girders (note the length of one over the nearest runner). It is in flame red/black livery with white lettering and BDA code. *Author's photo ref. W9111/DL*

No. 950868, taken at Cardiff Tidal Yard on 6 June 1992, is a Design Code BD006D BDA 80T steel carrier in original condition with a full complement of stanchions and loaded with steel reinforcing rods. It is in flame red/black livery with white lettering and BDA code. *Author's photo ref. W17071/DL*

Former identities of Lot 3965 vehicles: 950801 (B927092); 950802 (B942020); 950803 (B942646); 950804 (B942385); 950805 (B942772); 950806 (B927031); 950807 (B942870); 950808 (B927216); 950809 (B942692); 950810 (B927125); 950811 (B941976); 950812 (B942828); 950813 (B927048); 950814 (B942169); 950815 (B927172); 950816 (B941902); 950817 (B942721); 950818 (B927250); 950819 (B927061); 950820 (B942192); 950821 (B927232); 950822 (B942606); 950823 (B927242); 950824 (B942570); 950825 (B941759); 950826 (B927268); 950827 (B927090); 950828 (B927110); 950829 (B942076); 950830 (B942453); 950831 (B942075); 950832 (B941219); 950833 (B942354); 950834 (B941782); 950835 (B927177); 950836 (B942809); 950837 (B942277); 950838 (B942642); 950839 (B941463); 950840 (B941251); 950841 (B942527); 950842 (B942083); 950843 (B942432); 950844 (B942496); 950845 (B942523); 950846 (B941739); 950847 (B942724); 950848 (B942777); 950849 (B942197); 950850 (B942557); 950851 (B942202); 950852 (B941742); 950853 (B927153); 950854 (B942188); 950855 (B941626); 950856 (B942284); 950857 (B927245); 950858 (B927285); 950859 (B942296); 950860 (B942060); 950861 (B941926); 950862 (B942376); 950863 (B942065); 950864 (B927064); 950865 (B942121); 950866 (B942290); 950867 (B941988); 950868 (B942143); 950869 (B941338); 950870 (B942425); 950871 (B942129); 950872 (B942450); 950873 (B927219); 950874 (B927185); 950875 (B941977); 950876 (B941156); 950877 (B942317); 950878 (B927321); 950879 (B942329); 950880 (B941438); 950881 (B927083); 950882 (B941935); 950883 (B942015); 950884 (B941555); 950885 (B927340); 950886 (B942862); 950887 (B942698); 950888 (B927066); 950889 (B927320); 950890 (B927341); 950891 (B927390); 950892 (B927323); 950893 (B942446); 950894 (B927203); 950895 (B927222); 950896 (B927203); 950897 (B942735); 950898 (B942877); 950899 (B941999); 950900 (B941687)

950801 to 950850 were transferred to the CCE to become YAA BRILL. Others were rebuilt as BFA and BTA wagons (see pages 54/55 and 58 respectively for details).

Design Code BD006 80T GLW Bogie Steel Carrier Lot 3965 vehicles (as YAA BRILL)

No. DC950829, taken at Leyton CCE depot, Stratford, on 19 February 1989, is a Design Code BD006D BDA 80T steel carrier in original condition transferred to the CCE and loaded with scrap rails. It retains flame red/black livery with white lettering and YAA code and BRILL name. *Author's photo ref. W15036/DL*

No. DC950807, taken at Hither Green PAD on 5 May 1989, is a Design Code BD006D BDA 80T steel carrier in original condition transferred to the CCE and loaded with conductor rails. It has been repainted in yellow/grey livery with black lettering and BDA code and BRILL name. *Author's photo ref. W16416/DL*

Design Code BD006 80T GLW Bogie Steel Carrier Lot 3968 vehicles

No. 950915, taken at Southampton Bevois Park goods yard on 1 February 1989, is a Design Code BD006D BDA 80T steel carrier in original condition with a full complement of stanchions and loaded with steel H-girders. It is in flame red/black livery with white lettering and BDA code and double-arrow/Railfreight symbol. *Author's photo ref. W14915/DL*

No. 950963, taken at Severn Tunnel Junction Yard on 13 March 1983, is a Design Code BD006D BDA 80T steel carrier in original condition with a full complement of stanchions and loaded with steel bars. It is in flame red/black livery with white lettering and BDA code. *Author's photo ref. W12922/DL*

No. 950996, taken at Southampton Northam goods yard on 10 March 1989, is a Design Code BD006D BDA 80T steel carrier in original condition with a full complement of stanchions and loaded with steel reinforcing rods. It is in flame red/black livery with white lettering and BDA code. *Author's photo ref. W15501/DL*

Former identities of Lot 3968 vehicles: 950901 (B941541); 950902 (B941833); 950903 (B927322); 950904 (B941654); 950905 (B927178); 950906 (B941230); 950907 (B941614); 950908 (B942804); 950909 (B942692); 950910 (B941897); 950911 (B942053); 950912 (B942832); 950913 (B942144); 950914 (B942168); 950915 (B941402); 950916 (B927906); 950917 (B927355); 950918 (B941532); 950919 (B941238); 950920 (B942344); 950921 (B942452); 950922 (B942442); 950923 (B928169); 950924 (B927096); 950925 (B927557); 950926 (B927420); 950927 (B941171); 950928 (B927386); 950929 (B941937); 950930 (B941409); 950931 (B942855); 950932 (B941986); 950933 (B942514); 950934 (B927169); 950935 (B941641); 950936 (B942140); 950937 (B927077); 950938 (B942664); 950939 (B927293); 950940 (B927515); 950941 (B942013); 950942 (B942370); 950943 (B941643); 950944 (B942135); 950945 (B942640); 950946 (B941375); 950947 (B941170); 950948 (B927310); 950949 (B941660); 950950 (B942302); 950951 (B941151); 950952 (B927244); 950953 (B941452); 950954 (B941243); 950955 (B942788); 950956 (B942022); 950957 (B942087); 950958 (B942267); 950959 (B941984); 950960 (B927290); 950961 (B927099); 950962 (B941838); 950963 (B927367); 950964 (B941932); 950965 (B941165); 950966 (B941507); 950967 (B942397); 950968 (B942508); 950969 (B942625); 950970 (B942906); 950971 (B927330); 950972 (B942424); 950973 (B942556); 950974 (B927207); 950975 (B942716); 950976 (B941946); 950977 (B942377); 950978 (B941351); 950979 (B942170); 950980 (B941723); 950981 (B941265); 950982 (B942926); 950983 (B941193); 950984 (B941336); 950985 (B942307); 950986 (B942862); 950987 (B942698); 950988 (B927066); 950989 (B927320); 950990 (B927341); 950991 (B941182); 950992 (B942732);950993 (B941956); 950994 (B927165); 950995 (B927259); 950996 (B927215); 950997 (B941345); 950998 (B941744); 950999 (B941749); 951000 (B941644); 951001 (B942056); 951002 (B941726); 951003 (B941525); 951004 (B927354); 951005 (B941519); 951006 (B927243); 951007 (B927198); 951008 (B941854); 951009 (B942884); 951010 (B942526); 951011 (B942016); 951012 (B942411); 951013 (B942647); 951014 (B927395); 951015 (B942897); 951016 (B942353); 951017 (B941725); 951018 (B941363); 951019 (B942386); 951020 (B942215); 951021 (B927205); 951022 (B941811); 951023 (B942656); 951024 (B942620); 951025 (B942180); 951026 (B942289); 951027 (B941382); 951028 (B942655); 951029 (B942518); 951030 (B942235); 951031 (B942507); 951032 (B942051); 951033 (B942233); 951034 (B942226); 951035 (B942542); 951036 (B942896); 951037 (B941691); 951038 (B927274); 951039 (B941601); 951040 (B941465); 951041 (B941920); 951042 (B941548); 951043 (B941271); 951044 (B942166); 951045 (B941622); 951046 (B941313); 951047 (B942920); 951048 (B942011); 951049 (B942247); 951050 (B942034); 951051 (B941767); 951052 (B941177); 951053 (B942250); 951054 (B942695); 951055 (B942299); 951056 (B941928); 951057 (B941365); 951058 (B927373); 951059 (B941173); 951060 (B927182); 951061 (B927501); 951062 (B927442); 951063 (B941858); 951064 (B942911); 951065 (B942686); 951066 (B941187); 951067 (B942351); 951068 (B941503); 951069 (B941279); 951070 (B942260); 951071 (B941222); 951072 (B927881); 951073 (B941342); 951074 (B942554); 951075 (B941708); 951076 (unknown); 951077 (B941263); 951078 (B942232); 951079 (B927303); 951080 (B927700); 951081 (B942566); 951082 (B927925); 951083 (B941344); 951084

(B942551); 951085 (B942250); 951086 (B927643); 951087 (B941390); 951088 (B941699); 951089 (B941734); 951090 (B942402); 951091 (B941316); 951092 (B941864); 951093 (B941566); 951094 (B941214); 951095 (B927060); 951096 (B941657); 951097 (B941674); 951098 (B942323); 951099 (B941445); 951100 (B941181); 951101 (B942460); 951102 (B941458); 951103 (B941207); 951104 (B941686); 951105 (B927234); 951106 (B927953); 951107 (B941208); 951108 (B941464); 951109 (B927971); 951110 (B941350); 951111 (B941337); 951112 (B941990); 951113 (B927461); 951114 (B941692); 951115 (B942120); 951116 (B942222); 951117 (B941973); 951118 (B927041); 951119 (B941757); 951120 (B942665); 951121 (B942840); 951122 (B941658); 951123 (B941755); 951124 (B942904); 951125 (B927389); 951126 (B941433); 951127 (B927055); 951128 (B941705); 951129 (B941779); 951130 (B941916); 951131 (B941728); 951132 (B941327); 951133 (B941661); 951134 (B927068); 951135 (B942861); 951136 (B941970); 951137 (B942882); 951138 (B941675); 951139 (B927084); 951140 (B927464); 951141 (B927428); 951142 (B927562); 951143 (B941597); 951144 (B927351); 951145 (B942356); 951146 (B942146); 951147 (B941595); 951148 (B941584); 951149 (B941756); 951150 (B941655); 951151 (B941432); 951152 (B941624); 951153 (B941836); 951154 (B941459); 951155 (B942439); 951156 (B941217); 951157 (B927155); 951158 (B942913); 951159 (B941965); 951160 (B927057); 951161 (B927145); 951162 (B942348); 951163 (B942287); 951164 (B941740); 951165 (B941731); 951166 (B941185); 951167 (B942350); 951168 (B941851); 951169 (B941392); 951170 (B941416); 951171 (B941594); 951172 (B928144); 951173 (B942810); 951174 (B927628); 951175 (B942495); 951176 (B941769); 951177 (B941408); 951178 (B942359); 951179 (B941822); 951180 (B941781); 951181 (B927115); 951182 (B942463); 951183 (B941962); 951184 (B941549); 951185 (B941175); 951186 (B942321); 951187 (B941439); 951188 (B941841); 951189 (B941225); 951190 (B942596); 951191 (B941188); 951192 (B941488); 951193 (B942538); 951194 (B941378); 951195 (B941413); 951196 (B941924); 951197 (B942441); 951198 (B941423); 951199 (B942244); 951200 (B942073); 951201 (B941462); 951202 (B942710); 951203 (B941807); 951204 (B942172); 951205 (B942531); 951206 (B941748); 951207 (B942700); 951208 (B941529); 951209 (B941853); 951210 (B927095); 951211 (B927287); 951212 (B941262); 951213 (B927282); 951214 (B941713); 951215 (B941448); 951216 (B941754); 951217 (B942426); 951218 (B941552); 951219 (B941261); 951220 (B941703); 951221 (B927137); 951222 (B942179); 951223 (B942718); 951224 (B941487); 951225 (B941944); 951226 (B942061); 951227 (B941919); 951228 (B942384); 951229 (B941580); 951230 (B941168); 951231 (B942009); 951232 (B941359); 951233 (B941967); 951234 (B941771); 951235 (B941611); 951236 (B941324); 951237 (B942042); 951238 (B941353); 951239 (B942892); 951240 (B941903); 951241 (B927126); 951242 (B927043); 951243 (B927014); 951244 (B927336); 951245 (B942094); 951246 (B941855); 951247 (B942212); 951248 (B942025); 951249 (B942619); 951250 (B927100)

951251 to 951550 were ordered as part of Lot 3968 but were not built. This appears to have been due to the lack of suitable Diagram 1/472 BDOs as seven JMVs, which had been converted from vacuum-braked Bogie Bolster Ds, were substituted. These were 951080 (originally Diagram 1/478 B927700) and the remainder formerly Diagram 1/484, viz 950923 (B928169), 951072 (B927881), 951082 (B927923), 951106 (B927953), 951109 (927972) and 951172 (B928143).

No. 951095, taken at Hoo Junction Yard on 17 December 1988, is a Design Code BD006D BDA 80T steel carrier in original condition with a full complement of stanchions and loaded with steel U-section channel. It is in flame red/black livery with white lettering and BDA code and double-arrow symbol. *Author's photo ref. W14369/DL*

No. 951122, taken at Warrington Dallam goods yard on 23 October 1988, is a Design Code BD006D BDA 80T steel carrier in original condition with a full complement of stanchions and loaded with steel U-section channel, which is being unloaded. It is in flame red/black livery with white lettering and BDA code. *Author's photo ref. W14126/DL*

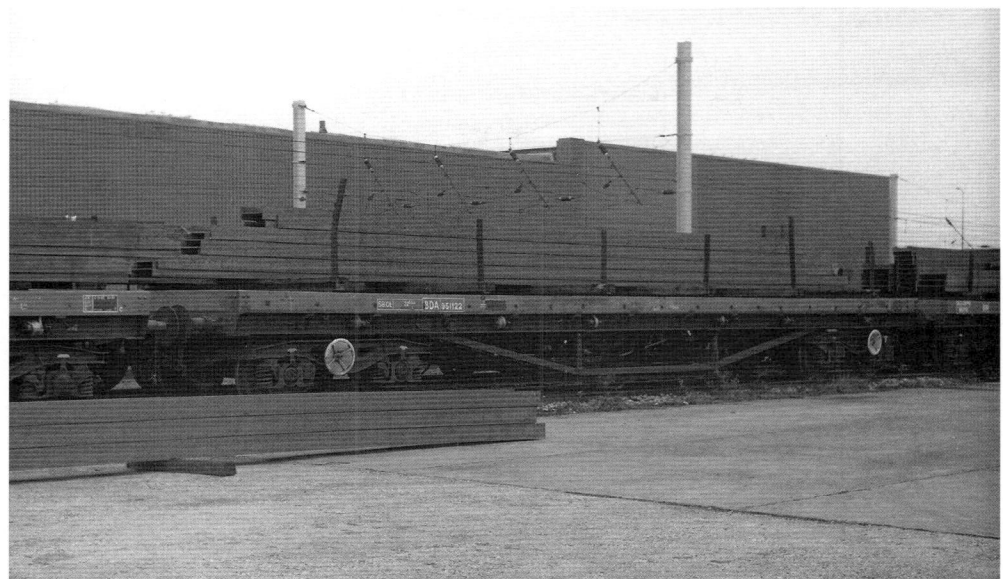

No. 951061, taken at Sheffield steel terminal on 22 October 1988, is a Design Code BD006D BDA 80T steel carrier in original condition with a full complement of stanchions and loaded with steel reinforcing rods. It is in flame red/black livery with white lettering and BDA code and double-arrow/Railfreight symbol. *Author's photo ref. W14097/DL*

No. 951191, taken at Hoo Junction Yard in August 1989, is a Design Code BD006D BDA 80T steel carrier in original condition with a full complement of stanchions and loaded with steel reinforcing rods. It is in flame red/black livery with white lettering and BDA code and double-arrow/Railfreight symbol. *Author's photo ref. W16437/DL*

No. 951221, taken at Severn Tunnel Junction Yard on 13 March 1983, is a Design Code BD006D BDA 80T steel carrier in original condition with a full complement of stanchions and loaded with steel H-girders. It is in flame red/black livery with white lettering and BDA code and double-arrow/Railfreight symbol. *Author's photo ref. W12905/DL*

No. 950689, taken at Rotherham steel terminal on 22 October 1988, is a Design Code BD006C BDA 80T steel carrier with modified bolsters and loaded with steel billets. It is in flame red/black livery with white lettering and BFA code and special 'B.S.C. SCUNTHORPE' lettering. *Author's photo ref. W14111/DL*

Design Code BD006 80T GLW Bogie Steel Carrier BDAs converted to BFA with modified bolsters to carry steel bars

This conversion allowed for special bolsters to be used to carry two tiers of steel billets, as seen in the view of 950661, from BSC, Scunthorpe works and appears to date from the late 1980s. Known numbers are as follows:

No. 950661, taken at Rotherham steel terminal on 22 October 1988, is a Design Code BD006C BDA 80T steel carrier with modified bolsters and loaded with steel billets. It is in freight brown livery with white lettering and BFA code and special 'B.S.C. SCUNTHORPE' lettering. *Author's photo ref. W14110/DL*

950370/2/5/80; 9950514/6/8/24/9/31/3-5/8/44-8/51/4/61/3/7/70/3-5/81/6/8/90/2/5-8; 950601/8/9/18/9/21/9/30/7/8/40/1/3/8/50/4/61/2/4/6-9/74/6/7/82/8/9/91/4/6/9; 950700/2/18/	9/34/6/70-2 (all from BD006C to BF002A) 950862/91; 950930/1/84; 951002/3 (all from BD006D to BF002A)

No. 950930, taken at Rotherham steel terminal on 22 October 1988, is a Design Code BD006D BDA 80T steel carrier with modified bolsters and loaded with steel billets. It is in flame red/black livery with white lettering and BFA code and special 'B.S.C. SCUNTHORPE' lettering. *Author's photo ref. W14119/DL*

Design Code BD006 80T GLW Bogie Steel Carrier BDAs converted to BMA with modified bolsters and new ends

This conversion was designated for aluminium ingots from Lynemouth and Fort William but the BMAs also appear to have carried other products. The conversion, which also involved BPA wagons, as detailed in Chapter 4, saw the recovery of BDAs from Lot 3907 which had been earmarked for the CCE as YAA BRILL together with a small number of others. Known numbers are as follows:

950003/7/12/3/6/20/1/3/5/8/32/9/43/51/8/62/5/9/70/73/5/9/80/3/9/9; 950101 /3/21/2/5/31/3/5/40-3/6/7/54/5/60/73/6/8/80/2/91/5/6/; 950200 (all from BD006B to BM002A, possibly via YAA001 BRILL)
950203; 950523/6/83; 950607/33; 950745/85/90 (all from BD006C to BM002A)
950833 (from BD006D to BM002A)

ABOVE No. 950195, taken at Tinsley Yard on 31 May 1992, is a Design Code BD006B BDA 80T steel carrier with modified bolsters and new ends. It is in flame red/black livery with white lettering and BMA code. *Author's photo ref. W17000/DL*

TOP RIGHT No. 950073, taken at Grimsby Docks on 29 May 1992, is a Design Code BD006B BDA 80T steel carrier converted to a BMA wagon and loaded with stainless steel slab for rolling after export. It is in flame red/black livery with white lettering and BMA code. *Author's photo ref. W16914/DL*

BOTTOM RIGHT No. 950012, taken at Grimsby Docks on 29 May 1992, is a Design Code BD006B BDA 80T steel carrier converted to a BMA wagon and loaded with stainless steel slab for rolling after export. It is in flame red/black livery with white lettering and BMA code. *Author's photo ref. W16919/DL*

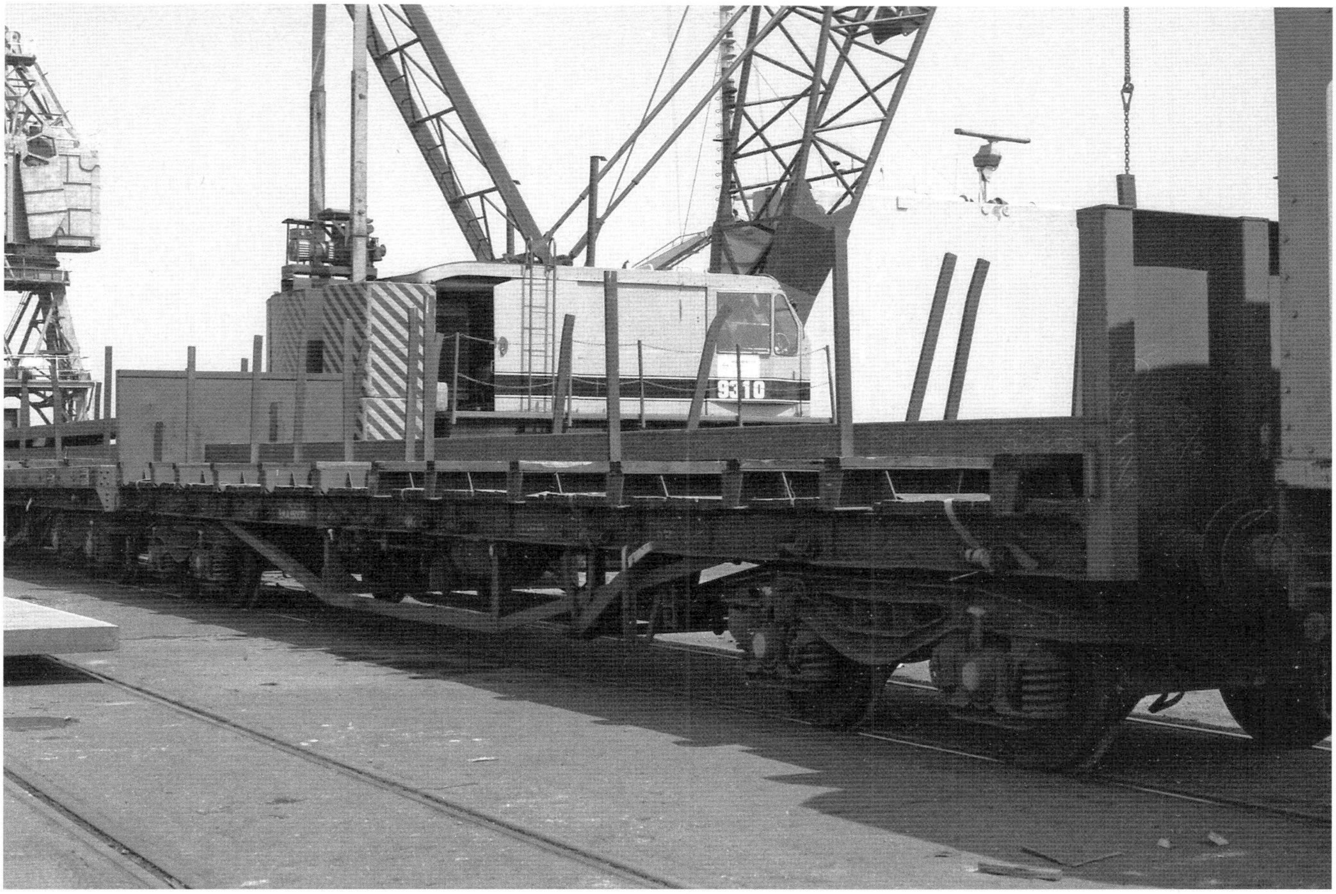
9310

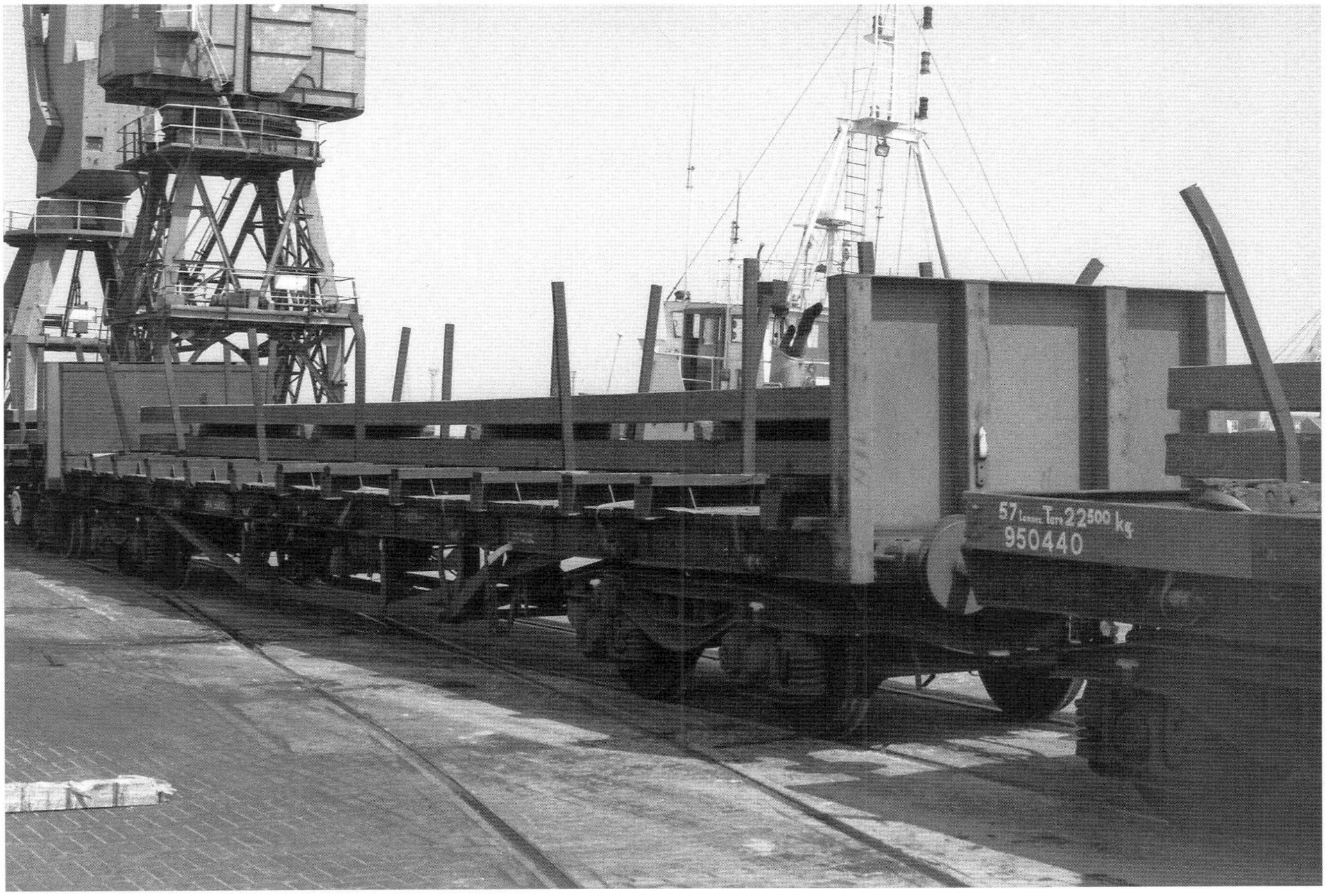
57 Tare 22500 kg
950440

Design Code BD006 80T GLW Bogie Steel Carrier BDAs converted to BTA with tall stanchions for logs

After the 1987 'hurricane', which brought down millions of trees, there was a need for wagons to transport the felled timber from the nearest railhead. A few BDAs, as seen in the view of 950191, formed part of the fleet and known numbers were as follows:

950017; 950123/91 (BD006B to BT003A); 950839 (BD006D to BT003A)

The timber, in log form, was carried in many converted wagons. Four-wheeled types, coded OTA, were the most numerous and came in a variety of shapes, being converted from OCA open wagons, details being found in Chapter 9, and from VDA vans, details being found in Chapter 12. Some of the traffic was also carried in unconverted OBA open wagons.

Bogie wagons were less numerous but, in addition to the BTAs seen in the view of 950123, some BDWs (vacuum-braked BDVs given air through-pipes) were also converted and are covered in Chapter 16.

No. 950191, taken at Dumfries goods yard on 6 June 1992, is a Design Code BD006C BDA converted to BT003A to convey timber in log form. It is in flame red/black livery with BTA code and Railfreight symbol. *Author's photo ref. W14204/DL*

No. 950123, taken at Dumfries goods yard on 6 June 1992, is a Design Code BD006C BDA converted to BT003A to convey timber in log form. It is in flame red/black livery with BTA code and Railfreight symbol. *Author's photo ref. W14203/DL*

4
Design Code BP004
BPA 58T Bogie Plate Wagon

965000 to 965049 – Converted to Lot 3985 by Shildon Works, May 1980 to July 1980.

965050 to 965079 – Converted to Lot 4011 by Shildon Works, May 1981 to June 1981; Design Code: BP004A; Length over headstocks: 52ft 0in; Length between bogie centres: 40ft 0in; Bogies: FBT 6 (Y25C); 3ft 1½in diameter wheels; Air brakes on bogies and disc hand-wheel on both bogies; 1ft 8½in Oleo Pneumatic Buffers; Roller bearings; Screw couplings; TOPS Code: BPA; No lettering carried.

These vehicles were all delivered in flame red/black livery. Some were transferred to the CCE as YNA wagons without a FISHKND name. Others were converted to BMA. Former identities are not available.

No. 965000, taken at Severn Tunnel Junction Yard on 5 November 1983, is a Design Code BP004A BPA 58T bogie plate wagon in original condition and loaded with rails. It is in weathered flame red/black livery with white lettering and BPA code. *Author's photo ref. W13410/DL*

No. 965015, taken at Toton Yard on 20 February 1983, is a Design Code BP004A BPA 58T bogie plate wagon in original condition. It is in flame red/black livery with white lettering and BPA code. *Author's photo ref. W12603/DL*

No. 965062, taken at Nunhead in July 1981, is a Design Code BP004A BPA 58T bogie plate wagon in original condition. It is in flame red/black livery with white lettering and BPA code. *Author's photo ref. W9119/DL*

No. 965065, taken at Whitehaven on 22 May 1982, is a Design Code BP004A BPA 58T bogie plate wagon in original condition. It is in flame red/black livery with white lettering and BPA code. *Author's photo ref. W11564/DL*

No. 965070, taken at Tees Yard in May 1981, is a Design Code BP004A BPA 58T bogie plate wagon in brand-new condition. It is in flame red/black livery with white lettering and BPA code. *Author's photo ref. W9121/DL*

Design Code BP004A 58T Bogie Plate Wagon – Wagons transferred to the CCE as YNA

The following wagons were transferred to the CCE department as Design Code YNA34B:

DC965000-25/7/8/30 (DC965003/4/6/10/14/5/7/20/3/4 later reverted to BPA)

LEFT No. DC965009, taken at Workington Yard on 16 June 1992, is a Design Code BP004A BPA 58T bogie plate wagon in original condition and transferred to the CCE as a YNA wagon. It is in yellow/black livery with black lettering and YNA code. *Author's photo ref. W17156/DL*

ABOVE No. DC965014, taken at Northwich yard on 26 May 1984, is a Design Code BP004A BPA 58T bogie plate wagon in original condition and transferred to the CCE as a YNA wagon. It is in weathered flame red/black livery with white lettering and YNA code. *Author's photo ref. W13931/DL*

LEFT No. DC965030, taken at Hoo Junction Yard on 12 January 1989, is a Design Code BP004A BPA 58T bogie plate wagon in original condition and transferred to the CCE as a YNA wagon. It is in weathered flame red/black livery with white lettering and YNA code. *Author's photo ref. W14819/DL*

Design Code BP004A 58T Bogie Plate Wagon – Wagons converted to BMA

As mentioned on page 56 when dealing with the identical BDA conversions, these BPAs were converted at the same time and performed the same duties. Known numbers were as follows:

965029/32/4/5/8-41/3/5-51/4/5/8-61/3-9/73/5-9

LEFT No. 965064, taken at Tinsley Yard on 31 May 1992, is a Design Code BP004A BPA 58T bogie plate wagon converted to a Design Code BM001A BMA wagon. It is in flame red/black livery with white lettering and BMA code. *Author's photo ref. W17003/DL*

No. 965059, taken at Grimsby Docks on 29 May 1992, is a Design Code BP004A BPA 58T bogie plate wagon converted to a BMA wagon and loaded with stainless steel slab for rolling after export. It is in flame red/black livery with white lettering and BMA code. *Author's photo ref. W16916/DL*

No. 965076, taken at Grimsby Docks on 29 May 1992, is a Design Code BP004A BPA 58T bogie plate wagon converted to a BMA wagon and loaded with stainless steel slab for rolling after export. It is in flame red/black livery with white lettering and BMA code. *Author's photo ref. W16920/DL*

5
Design Code BR006
BRA 49T Borail Wagon

967500 to 967649 – Converted to Lot 4012 by Shildon Works, July 1981 to January 1982; Design Code: BR006A; Length over headstocks: 62ft 0in; Length between bogie centres: 47ft 0in; Bogies: FBT 6 (Y25C); 3ft 1½in diameter wheels; Air brakes on bogies and disc hand-wheel on both bogies; 1ft 8½in Oleo Pneumatic Buffers; Roller bearings; Screw couplings; TOPS Code: BRA; No lettering carried.

These vehicles were all delivered in flame red/black livery. All were transferred to the CCE as YLA wagons with FISHKND name MULLET. Some were later converted to YMA wagons with FISHKND name PARR.

No. 967517, taken at Dewsnap Yard on 21 February 1982, is a Design Code BR006A BRA 49T bogie rail wagon in original condition and with loaded with rails. It is in flame red/black livery with white lettering and BRA code. *Author's photo ref. W11232/DL*

No. 967544, taken at Hoo Junction Yard in October 1981, is a Design Code BR006A BRA 49T bogie rail wagon in original condition and loaded with rails. It is in flame red/black livery with white lettering and BRA code. *Author's photo ref. W11193/DL*

No. 967554, taken at Burton-upon-Trent Yard on 12 September 1982, is a Design Code BR006A BRA 49T bogie rail wagon in original condition and with loaded with pointwork. It is in flame red/black livery with white lettering and BRA code. *Author's photo ref. W11885/DL*

No. 967580, taken at Warrington Arpley Yard on 20 February 1982, is a Design Code BR006A BRA 49T bogie rail wagon in original condition. It is in flame red/black livery with white lettering and BRA code. *Author's photo ref. W11221/DL*

No. 967628, taken at Workington Yard on 22 May 1982, is a Design Code BR006A BRA 49T bogie rail wagon in original condition. It is in flame red/black livery with white lettering and BRA code. *Author's photo ref. W11555/DL*

Design Code BR006A 49T Borail Wagon – Wagons transferred to the CCE as YLA MULLET

The whole BRA fleet was transferred to the CCE fairly quickly in 1983, although repainting in CCE yellow/black livery took some while. It is not known how common the loading seen above was but the wagons were not permanently coupled.

Wagons remaining as YLA MULLET were as follows:

DC967501/4-6/9-13/5/6/8/20-2/4/5/8/31/2/6/7/9/43-7/50/3/9/60/3/70/2/5/6/8/9/82-4/6-93/5-8; DC97600/2-8/10/2-4/7/9-21/4-38/40/1/8

Nos. DC967512 and DC967520, taken at Warrington Walton Old Junction Yard on 23 October 1988, are Design Code BP006A BRA 49T bogie rail wagons transferred to the CCE as YLA MULLET and loaded with extra-long rails. They are in yellow/black livery with black lettering and YLA code and MULLET name. *Author's photo ref. W14148/DL*

No. DC967600, taken at York Dringhouses Yard on 16 April 1983, is a Design Code BR006A BRA 49T bogie rail wagon in original condition and transferred to the CCE and loaded with rails. It retains flame red/black livery with white lettering and YLA code and FISHKND name MULLET on yellow patch. *Authors photo ref. W13031/DL*

ABOVE Nos. DC967618 and DC967635, taken at Warrington Walton Old Junction Yard on 23 October 1988, are Design Code BP006A BRA 49T bogie rail wagons transferred to the CCE as YLA MULLET and loaded with extra-long rails. They retain flame red/black livery with white lettering and YLA code and FISHKND name MULLET on yellow patch. *Author's photo ref. W14150/DL*

RIGHT No. DC967536, taken at Warrington Arpley Yard on 23 October 1988, is a Design Code BR006A BRA 49T bogie rail wagon in original condition and transferred to the CCE. It is in yellow/black livery with black lettering and YLA code and FISHKND name MULLET. *Author's photo ref. W14134/DL*

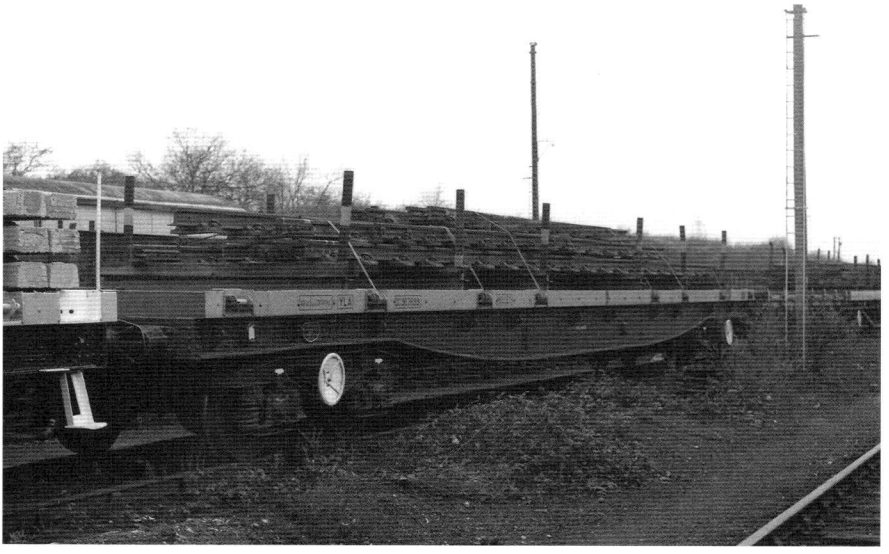

RIGHT No. DC967639, taken at Hoo Junction Yard on 31 December 1988, is a Design Code BR006A BRA 49T bogie rail wagon in original condition and transferred to the CCE and loaded with rails. It is in yellow/black livery with black lettering and YLA code and FISHKND name MULLET. *Author's photo ref. W14675/DL*

Design Code BR006A 49T Borail Wagon – Wagons as YLA MULLET converted to YMA PARR

Wagons converted to FISHKND PARR with bolsters removed to carry concrete sleepers were as follows:

YMA (YM002A): DC967500/3/7/17/9/23/6/7/9/30/5/8/40/2/54/61/73/4/85/99; DC97601/9/15/6/23/39/42-6
YQA (YQ001A): DC967502/8/14/33/4/41/8/51/2/5-8/62/4-9/71/7/80/1/94; DC967611/8/47/9

Initially the YMA (Design Code YM002A) was used but this was later changed, on TOPS initially if not on the wagon itself, to YQA (YQ001A).

BELOW No. DC967568, taken at Hoo Junction Yard on 31 December 1988, is a Design Code BR004A BRA 49T bogie rail wagon transferred to the CCE as YLA MULLET and converted to carry concrete sleepers as YMA PARR. It is in yellow/grey ends/black livery with black lettering and YMA code and PARR FISHKND name. *Author's photo ref. W14677/DL*

ABOVE No. DC967538, taken at Hoo Junction Yard on 31 December 1988, is a Design Code BR004A BRA 49T bogie rail wagon transferred to the CCE as YLA MULLET and converted to carry concrete sleepers as YQA PARR. It is in yellow/grey ends/black livery with black lettering and YQA code and PARR FISHKND name. *Author's photo ref. W14676/DL*

No. DC967533, taken at London Bridge station on 24 March 1989, is a Design Code BR004A BRA 49T bogie rail wagon transferred to the CCE as YLA MULLET and converted to carry concrete sleepers as YQA PARR. It is in yellow/grey ends/black livery with black lettering and YQA code and PARR FISHKND name. *Author's photo ref. W15982/DL*

6
Design Code FN003 FNA 50T Flatrol Nuclear Flask Wagon

Due to lack of photographic coverage, this chapter will be less comprehensive than the others. Changes in the way nuclear waste in flasks was carried occurred throughout the Speedlink period. The view of 550000 shows their appearance at the time of building but this may have changed before their withdrawal by 1991 (see also 550004 on page 72).

Their predecessors were still in operation in the early 1980s, as shown on page 71, and had received new bogies. Details of this batch were as follows:

B900509 to B900532 – 50T FLATROL MJ: Built to Lot 3300 to Diagram 2/532 by Swindon Works, from January 1961 to December 1963.

No. 550000, taken at Trawsfynydd loading point in April 1971, is a Diagram 2/534 50T FLATROL MJJ wagon in original condition. It is in freight brown livery with white lettering and FLATROL MJJ code. *Author's photo ref. W3413/DL*

Nos. B900513 (above) and B900520 (below), taken at Warrington Walton Old Junction Yard on 20 February 1982, show the condition of the Lot 3300 vehicles at that time. Both were in black livery with white shields, flask and lettering. Code was XKB. *Author's photo ref. W11017/Author's photo ref. W11222/DL*

No. 550004, taken at Warrington Walton Old Junction Yard on 20 February 1982, is an XKB Diagram 2/534 50T nuclear flask wagon. It is in an unusual blue livery with white XKB code and lettering. *Author's photo ref. W11016/DL*

It is not known how many others from this batch were in this condition or how long any survived in service.

550000 to 550005 – Built to Lot 3697 by Shildon Works, July 1981 to January 1982; Diagram 2/534; Length over headstocks: 37ft 0in; Length between bogie centres: 23ft 6in; Bogies: Gloucester; 3ft 1½in diameter wheels; Air brakes on bogies, Vacuum through-pipes and disc hand-wheel on ends; 1ft 8½in Oleo Pneumatic Buffers; Roller bearings; Instanter couplings; TOPS Code: XKB; No lettering carried.

It is not known why the sunshield is not over the flask in the view of 550004 but, as the latter look brandnew on this wagon and the two on page 71, they may have been on delivery unused.

550009 to 550014 – Built to Lot 3886 by Ashford Works, July 1981 to January 1982.
550015 to 550016 – Built to Lot 3928 by Ashford Works, November 1978 to January 1979.
Diagram 2/536, Design Code XK003A; Length over headstocks: 37ft 0in; Length between bogie centres: 23ft 6in; Bogies: FBT 6 (Y25C); 3ft 1½in diameter wheels; Air brakes on bogies, Vacuum through-pipes and disc hand-wheel on ends; 1ft 8½in Oleo Pneumatic Buffers; Roller bearings; Instanter couplings; TOPS Code: XKB; No lettering carried.

As built, these two Lots do not appear to have had sun shields and the original shape can be seen in the view of 550012 at Shildon.

550017 to 550018 – Built to Lot 4004 by Shildon Works, May 1982.
550019 to 550020 – Built to Lot 4040 by Swindon Works, 1986.
550021 to 550026 – Built to Lot 4049 by Swindon Works, 1986.
550027 to 550050 – Built to Lot 4063 by Procor (UK) Ltd, 1988.
Design Code XK003A; Length over headstocks: 37ft 0in; Length between bogie centres: 23ft 6in; Bogies: FBT 6 (Y25C); 3ft 1½in diameter wheels; Air brakes on bogies and disc hand-wheel on ends; 1ft 8½in Oleo Pneumatic Buffers; Roller bearings; Instanter couplings; TOPS Code: XKB; No lettering carried.

It is thought all the above wagons were of this design and had reached 550058 by the end of Speedlink.

No. 550012, taken at Shildon Works in September 1981, is a Lot 3886 XKB Diagram 50T nuclear flask wagon under conversion to an FNA. It is in buff livery with white XKB code and lettering. *Author's photo ref. W10015/DL*

No. 550012, taken at Hither Green station on 9 July 1992, is a Lot 3886 XKB Diagram 50T nuclear flask wagon after conversion to an FNA. It is in buff livery with white sunshield, white FNA code and lettering on black panels. *Author's photo ref. W17273/DL*

No. 550018, taken at Hither Green station on 25 June 1992, is a Lot 4004 Design Code FN003A 50T FNA nuclear flask wagon. It is in buff livery with white sunshield, white FNA code and lettering on black panels. *Author's photo ref. W17256/DL*

No. 550058, taken at Hither Green station on 25 June 1992, is a Procor-built Design Code FN003F 50T FNA nuclear flask wagon. It is in buff livery with white sunshield, white FNA code and lettering on black panels. *Author's photo ref. W17255/DL*

7
Design Code HB001
HBA 46T Hopper Mineral Wagon

360001 to 361998 – Built to Lot 3885 by Shildon Works, September 1976 to March 1979; Design Code: HB001A; Length over headstocks: 24ft 3in; Wheelbase: 15ft 0in; Springs: Long Link; 3ft 1½in diameter wheels; Air disc brakes and hand lever; 1ft 7in Oleo Pneumatic Buffers; Roller bearings; Instanter couplings; TOPS Code: HBA; No lettering carried.

This batch was built with long link suspension but received Brueninghaus springs later, being recoded HEA. The last two wagons from the batch (361999 and 362000) were built as MFA wagons (see Chapter 16 for details). Other conversions were to RNA nuclear flask barrier wagons (see page 90/91) and SJA scrap wagons (see page 92). There were later conversions after the demise of Speedlink.

No. 360111, taken at Hoo Junction Yard in February 1978, is a Design Code HB001A HBA 46T GLW mineral hopper wagon in original condition. It is in freight brown livery with white lettering and HBA code. *Author's photo ref. W6997/DL*

Design Code HB001 46T Hopper Wagon Mineral – Early wagons (up to approximately 360226) with central end ladders

The position of the ladder appears to have been moved from the centre to the left-hand end because it was immediately above the coupling hook and therefore difficult to access.

No. 360182, taken at Birkenhead Docks in February 1980, is an HBA hopper mineral wagon with central ladder in original condition. It is in freight brown livery with white lettering and HBA code. *Author's photo ref. W8682/DL*

No. 360204, taken at Birkenhead Docks in February 1980, is an HBA hopper mineral wagon with central ladder in original condition. It is in freshly repainted flame red/grey/black livery with white lettering, HBA code and unboxed double-arrow/Railfreight symbol. *Author's photo ref. W8683/DL*

Design Code HB001 46T Hopper Wagon Mineral – Early wagons (up to approximately 360226) as HEA with new springs

No. 360008, taken at Whitwell Colliery, Bolsover, on 19 February 1983, is an HBA hopper mineral wagon with central ladder resprung as an HEA. It is in freight brown livery with white lettering and HEA code. *Author's photo ref. W12516/DL*

No. 360008, taken at Whitwell Colliery, Bolsover, on 19 February 1983, is an HBA hopper mineral wagon with central ladder resprung as an HEA. It is in freight brown livery with white lettering and HEA code. *Author's photo ref. W12516/DL*

No. 360001, taken at Whitwell Colliery, Bolsover, on 19 February 1983, is an HBA hopper mineral wagon with central ladder resprung as an HEA. It is in repainted flame red/grey/black livery with white lettering, HEA code and boxed double-arrow/Railfreight symbol. *Author's photo ref. W12515/DL*

Design Code HB001 46T Hopper Wagon Mineral – Early wagons (up to approximately 360226) as HSA Scrap wagon

No. 360040, taken at Manchester Ardwick East on 24 October 1988, is an HBA hopper mineral wagon with central ladder, resprung as an HEA and recoded as an HSA scrap wagon. It is in freight brown livery with white lettering and HSA code. *Author's photo ref. W14168/DL*

No. 360149, taken at Manchester Ardwick East on 24 October 1988, is an HBA hopper mineral wagon with central ladder, resprung as an HEA and recoded as an HSA scrap wagon. It is in repainted flame red/grey/black livery with white lettering, HBA code and boxed double-arrow/Railfreight symbol. *Author's photo ref. W14165/DL*

Design Code HB001 46T Hopper Wagon Mineral – Main batch wagons with original springs as HBA

With the position of the ladder now moved, the step on the right of the buffer beam was moved to the left and the grab handles were removed, as seen opposite. The wagons, such as 360618 illustrated, were kept at Hoo Junction to carry the oil tail lamps then in use on railtanks carrying Class A loads or liquid petroleum gases. Wagons repainted in flame red/grey/black livery appear with a variety of symbol styles.

RIGHT No. 360618, taken at Hoo Junction Yard in December 1977, is a Design Code HB001A HBA 46T mineral hopper wagon in brand-new condition. It is in freight brown/black livery with white lettering and HBA code. *Author's photo ref. W8688/DL*

ABOVE No. 360283, taken at Birkenhead Docks in February 1980, is an HBA hopper mineral wagon in original condition. It is in freshly repainted flame red/grey/black livery with white lettering, HBA code and boxed double-arrow/Railfreight symbol. *Author's photo ref. W8684/DL*

LEFT No. 361733, taken at Birkenhead Docks in February 1980, is an HBA hopper mineral wagon in original condition. It is in freight brown livery with white lettering and HBA code. *Author's photo ref. W8695B/DL*

No. 360320, taken at Birkenhead Docks in February 1980, is an HBA hopper mineral wagon in original condition. It is in freshly repainted flame red/grey/black livery with white lettering, HBA code and small boxed double-arrow/Railfreight symbol. *Author's photo ref. W8685/DL*

No. 360712, taken at Birkenhead Docks in February 1980, is an HBA hopper mineral wagon in original condition. It is in freshly repainted flame red/grey/black livery with white lettering, HBA code and unboxed double-arrow/Railfreight symbol. *Author's photo ref. W8689/DL*

Design Code HB001 46T Hopper Wagon Mineral – Main batch wagons as HEA with new springs

No. 360374, taken at Avonmouth Docks on 11 March 1989, is an HBA hopper mineral wagon resprung as an HEA. It is in freight brown livery with white lettering and HEA code. *Author's photo ref. W15709/DL*

No. 361366, taken at Bow goods yard, London, on 19 February 1989, is an HBA hopper mineral wagon resprung as an HEA. It is in freight brown livery with white lettering and HEA code. *Author's photo ref. W14993/DL*

No. 361338, taken at Avonmouth goods yard on 11 March 1989, is an HBA hopper mineral wagon resprung as an HEA. It is in flame red/grey/black livery with white lettering, HEA code and small boxed double-arrow/Railfreight symbol. *Author's photo ref. W15712/DL*

No. 360275, taken at Avonmouth goods yard on 11 March 1989, is an HBA hopper mineral wagon resprung as an HEA. It is in flame red/grey/black livery with white lettering, HEA code and boxed double-arrow/Railfreight symbol. *Author's photo ref. W15707/DL*

Design Code HB001 46T Hopper Wagon Mineral – Main batch wagons (Livery and Spring variants)

RIGHT No. 360879, taken at Maidstone West goods yard on an exhibition train in September 1977, is an HBA hopper mineral wagon in original condition. It is in freight brown livery with white lettering, HBA code and double-arrow/Railfreight symbol. *Author's photo ref. W8692/DL*

BELOW No. 361714, taken at Temple Mills Yard on a livery demonstration train in August 1979, is an HBA hopper mineral wagon in original condition. It is in flame red/black livery without grey frames but with white lettering, HBA code and double-arrow/Railfreight symbol. *Author's photo ref. W7786/DL*

No. 361552, taken at Whitwell Colliery, Bolsover, on 19 March 1983, is an HBA hopper mineral wagon in original condition. It is in flame red/grey/black livery with white lettering, HEA code and double-arrow/Railfreight symbol in an unusual position. *Author's photo ref. W12513/DL*

ABOVE No. 361786, taken at Nunhead in July 1981, is an HBA hopper mineral wagon in original condition with vertical-link Brueninghaus springs. It is in orange livery with white lettering and HBA code on black panels. *Author's photo ref. W8988B/DL*

RIGHT No. 360955, taken at Toton Yard on 1 March 1983, is an HBA hopper mineral wagon in original condition with Gloucester floating axle springs. It is in flame red/grey/black livery with white lettering, HEA code and small double-arrow/Railfreight symbol. *Author's photo ref. W12926A/DL*

RIGHT No. 361785, taken at Birkenhead Docks in February 1980, is an HBA hopper mineral wagon with experimental Brueninghaus suspension. It is in freight brown livery with white lettering and HBA code. *Author's photo ref. W8699/DL*

Design Code HB001 46T Hopper Wagon Mineral – Main batch wagons (later wagons with *Brueninghaus* springs)

The exact point when new vehicles with Brueninghaus springs began to be delivered is approximately 361800 but they came out initially with the HBA code almost to 361998.

The fleet was involved in a number of conversions, such as the HSA, the RNA and SJA and these will be examined on pages 87-92. However, see page 78 for two HSAs from the first batch with central ladders.

LEFT No. 361885, taken at Birkenhead Docks in February 1980, is an HBA hopper mineral wagon in original condition. It is in freight brown livery with white lettering and HBA code. *Author's photo ref. W8701A/DL*

BELOW No. 361945, taken at Strood goods yard on 8 March 1983, is an HBA hopper mineral wagon in original condition. It is in flame red/grey/black livery with white lettering, with new HEA code and small boxed double-arrow/Railfreight symbol. *Author's photo ref. W12705/DL*

No. 361812, taken at Hartlepools yard in September 1981, is an HBA hopper mineral wagon in original condition. It is in repainted flame red/grey/black livery with white lettering but retaining the HBA code. *Author's photo ref. W8989/DL*

Design Code HB001 46T Hopper Wagon Mineral – Main batch wagons in RfD Sector livery

No. 360853, taken at Peak Forest on 23 February 1989, is an HBA hopper mineral wagon, resprung as an HEA. It is in Sector dark grey/yellow livery with white lettering, HEA code and RfD Sector symbol. *Author's photo ref. W15308/DL*

No. 361870, taken at Peak Forest on 23 February 1989, is an HBA hopper mineral wagon in original condition and recoded as an HEA. It is in Sector dark grey/yellow livery with white lettering, HEA code and RfD Sector symbol. *Author's photo ref. W15307/DL*

Design Code HB001 46T Hopper Wagon Mineral – Main batch wagons (HSA Scrap wagons)

This conversion was carried out in 1987 when 131 redundant HEAs had the bottom doors plated over. Externally the only visual change was the change of code to HSA and known numbers were as follows:

No. 360353, taken at Manchester Ardwick East on 24 October 1988, is an HBA hopper mineral wagon, resprung as an HEA and recoded as an HSA scrap wagon. It is in freight brown livery with white lettering and HSA code. *Author's photo ref. W14181/DL*

360008/19/21/40/71/3/5/8/87/97; 360122-4/7/35/9/43/5/9/ 63/9/73/7/9/83/92; 360215/6/8/36/51/2/60/5/7/87; 360311/ 2/20/9/33/9/51/3/7/8 /71/91; 360422/4 /51/4/7/8/60/6/77; 360500/2/11/27/32/7/9/41/2/4/8/72/95; 360600/3/13/5/6/27 39 /49/52/64/5; 360702/7/13/28/9/31/7/43/8/66/81/5/8/94; 360802/16/7/20/6/9/40/7 /50/63/5/74; 360902/4/13/4/24/9/ 48/58/69/73/82/92-4; 361038/46/57/61/82-4 /92/4/9; 361103/31-3/44/55/8/65/72/86/7/94/9; 361200/9/10/26/7/ 37/52/7/69/78 /84/6/8; 361304/9-12/9/24/33/44/54/68/84/ 5/9/95/9; 361414/21/6/32-4/7/9/82/3/93; 361509/25/6/38/ 44/5/9/83/92; 361618/22/4/34/46/8/59/61/84/9/93; 361702/ 14/26 /31/41/9/50/8/66/73/7/85/92/6; 361800/4/34/45/54/5/ 9/64/71/80/95; 361901 /12/9/35/9/41/63/5/98

Three wagons were rebodied with new bodywork to become SJA (see page 92 for details).

BELOW No. 360600, taken at Manchester Ardwick East on 24 October 1988, is an HBA hopper mineral wagon, resprung as an HEA and recoded as an HSA scrap wagon. It is in freight brown livery with white lettering and HSA code. *Author's photo ref. W14182/DL*

No. 361187, taken at Manchester Ardwick East on 24 October 1988, is an HBA hopper mineral wagon, resprung as an HEA and recoded as an HSA scrap wagon. It is in freight brown livery with white lettering and HSA code. *Author's photo ref. W14167/DL*

No. 361758, taken at Manchester Ardwick East on 24 October 1988, is an HBA hopper mineral wagon, resprung as an HEA and recoded as an HSA scrap wagon. It is in flame red/grey/black livery with white lettering, HSA code and small boxed double-arrow/Railfreight symbol. *Author's photo ref. W14169/DL*

No. 361312, taken at Manchester Ardwick East on 24 October 1988, is an HBA hopper mineral wagon, resprung as an HEA and recoded as an HSA scrap wagon. It is in flame red/grey/black livery with white lettering, HSA code and small boxed double-arrow/Railfreight symbol. *Author's photo ref. W14164/DL*

Design Code HB001 46T Hopper Wagon Mineral – Main batch wagons (RNA Nuclear Barrier wagons)

This re-allocation, followed by a conversion, involved wagons dedicated to act as barrier wagons on either side of nuclear flask wagons. Initially, this merely involved a change of TOPS code but eventually the bodywork was cut down. Known numbers were as follows, although it cannot be confirmed as to which ones were cut down:

360046/69; 360211; 360323; 360492; 360592; 360610/30; 360716/39/68; 360808; 361001; 361105/12/84; 361253/74; 361394; 361484; 361522/61/81; 361627; 361738/9/74/98; 361867; 361900/10 /68/90

Wagons known to be cut down are 360592, 361001, 361164, 361484, 361739/98 and 361900.

No. 361990, taken at Hither Green station on 25 June 1992, is an HBA hopper mineral wagon resprung as an HEA and recoded as an RNA nuclear barrier wagon. It is in flame red/grey/black livery with white lettering, RNA code and small boxed double-arrow/Railfreight symbol. *Author's photo ref. W17257/DL*

No. 360323, taken at Hither Green station on 25 June 1992, is an HBA hopper mineral wagon resprung as an HEA and recoded as an RNA nuclear barrier wagon. It is in freight brown livery with white lettering and RNA code. *Author's photo ref. W17254/DL*

No. 360610, taken at Hither Green Yard on 26 July 1992, is an HBA hopper mineral wagon resprung and with vacuum through-pipe and recoded as an RNB nuclear barrier wagon. It is in dark grey/yellow Sector livery with white lettering, RNA code and Coal Sector symbol. *Author's photo ref. W17294/DL*

No. 360323, taken at Hither Green station on 25 June 1992, is an HBA hopper mineral wagon resprung as an HEA and cut down as an RNA nuclear barrier wagon. It is in freight brown livery with white lettering and RNA code. *Author's photo ref. W17195/DL*

No. 361798, taken at Carlisle Currock C&W depot (after withdrawal) on 16 June 1992, is an HBA hopper mineral wagon with vertical-link Brueninghaus suspension and cut down as an RNA nuclear barrier wagon. It is in dark grey/yellow Sector livery with white lettering, RNA code and Coal Sector symbol. *Author's photo ref. W17180/DL*

No. 361001, taken at Hither Green station on 2 July 1992, is an HBA hopper mineral wagon resprung as an HEA and cut down as an RNA nuclear barrier wagon. It is in dark grey/yellow Sector livery with white lettering, RNA code and Coal Sector symbol. *Author's photo ref. W17270/DL*

No. 361484, taken at Hither Green station on 2 July 1992, is an HBA hopper mineral wagon resprung as an HEA and cut down as an RNA nuclear barrier wagon. It is in dark grey/yellow Sector livery with white lettering, RNA code and Coal Sector symbol. *Author's photo ref. W17272/DL*

Design Code HB001 46T Hopper Wagon Mineral – Box-bodied Scrap wagons (SJA)

As mentioned on page 87, three of the HEAs re-coded HSA for scrap traffic were rebuilt as SJA wagons, as seen on this page, in 1989. These wagons were numbered as follows:

360040, 360761, 361486

Although successful, they were not repeated and BR chose instead to purchase second-hand wagons, which were coded SSA (see page 93). The other HEA rebuilds, the MEAs, were Coal Sector wagons after the demise of Speedlink and thus not covered in this volume.

ABOVE No. 361486, taken at Tinsley Yard on 31 May 1992, is an HBA resprung as an HEA and converted to an SJA. Livery is flame red/black with white lettering and SJA code. *Author's photo ref. W16996/DL*

LEFT No. 360040, taken at Tinsley Yard on 31 May 1992, is an HBA resprung as an HEA and converted to an SJA. Livery is flame red/black with white lettering and SJA code. *Author's photo ref. W16995/DL*

LEFT No. 360761, taken at Tinsley Yard on 31 May 1992, is an HBA resprung as an HEA and converted to an SJA. Livery is flame red/black with white lettering and SJA code. *Author's photo ref. W16994/DL*

Design Code HB001 46T Hopper Wagon Mineral – Second-hand Box-bodied Scrap wagons (SSA) (SS002A)

Details were as follows:

470000 to 470099 – Design Code SS002A

No. 470057, taken at Tinsley Yard on 31 May 1992, is a second-hand POA RLS5057 sold to be an SSA. Livery is weathered pale blue/yellow with white lettering and SSA code. *Author's photo ref. W16992/DL*

No. 470087, taken at Tinsley Yard on 31 May 1992, is a second-hand POA RLS5087 sold to be an SSA. Livery is weathered pale blue/yellow with white lettering and SSA code. *Author's photo ref. W16987/DL*

Design Code HB001 46T Hopper Wagon Mineral – Second-hand Box-bodied Scrap wagons (SSA) (SS001)

Details were as follows:

470101 to 470120 – Design Code SS001B
470121 to 470150 – Design Code SS001C
470151 to 470180 – Design Code SS001D

Full details of these SSA wagons, including their origins, will be given in the volume in this series that deals with privately owned wagons.

No. 470103, taken at Tinsley Yard on 31 May 1992, is a second-hand POA RLS5903 sold to be an SSA. Livery is weathered pale blue/yellow with white lettering and SSA code. *Author's photo ref. W16990/DL*

No. 470130, taken at Tinsley Yard on 31 May 1992, is a second-hand POA RLS5930 sold to be an SSA. Livery is weathered pale blue/yellow with white lettering and SSA code. *Author's photo ref. W16986/DL*

No. 470169, taken at Tinsley Yard on 31 May 1992, is a second-hand POA RLS5969 sold to be an SSA. Livery is weathered pale blue/yellow with white lettering and SSA code. *Author's photo ref. W16985/DL*

8
Design Code OB001
OBA 46T Open Goods Wagon

110000 – Converted to Lot 3861 by Shildon Works, 1974; Design Code: OB001A; Length over headstocks: 33ft 6in; Wheelbase: 20ft 9in; Springs: Long Link; 3ft 1½in diameter wheels; Air disc brakes and hand lever; 1ft 8½in Oleo Pneumatic Buffers; Roller bearings; Screw couplings; TOPS Code: OBA; double-arrow/Railfreight symbol carried.

This wagon was a conversion of OPEN AB 100043 and was possibly released from works as 450000, an SDA Tube Wagon (45 tonnes GLW) to Design Code SD001A. It became the prototype OBA wagon. A view from the opposite side is below.

The chief differences between the original OPEN AB/OAA design and the OBA were the sides. On the former, these were three-part dropsides and, on the OBA, these became four-part

ABOVE No. 110000, taken at New Cross Gate CCE yard on 15 September 1982, is a Design Code OB001A OBA 46T GLW open wagon in original condition. It is in maroon livery with white lettering, OBA code and double-arrow/Railfreight symbol. *Author's photo ref. W11918A/DL*

LEFT No. 110000, taken at New Cross Gate CCE yard on 15 September 1982, is a Design Code OB001A OBA 46T GLW open wagon in original condition. It is in maroon livery with white lettering, OBA code and double-arrow/Railfreight symbol. *Author's photo ref. W11918B/DL*

Speedlink

No. DC110000, taken at Hither Green PAD on 19 March 1989, is a Design Code OB001A OBA 46T GLW open wagon in original condition and transferred to the CCE. It is in yellow/grey livery with white and black lettering, ZDA code and BASS name. *Author's photo ref. W15905/DL*

dropsides with removable dividers, which could be extended upwards to conform to the height of the new raised ends. On 110000 only, this end was hinged outwards and could be folded down to be the same height as the sides.

As were many other OBA wagons, this prototype wagon was transferred to the CCE as a ZDA BASS wagon to Design Code ZD143B.

The production batches of the OBA type, to Lots 3909 and 3930, retained the four-part drop sides, with removable and extendable dividers but had fixed ends. As well as transfers to the CCE, there were conversions for Plasmor traffic (Design Code OB001E) and full re-buildings to OTA timber wagons and RRA Runner wagons. 110486 to 110514 were sold to become BNFL91000 to BNFL91029 for low-grade nuclear waste but, because they only worked between Sellafield and Drigg, are not part of the Speedlink story.

No. 110017, taken at Longhedge Junction, Battersea, in March 1977, is a Design Code OB001B OBA 46T GLW open wagon in original condition. It is in maroon livery with white lettering, OBA code and double-arrow/Railfreight symbol. *Author's photo ref. W7352/DL*

Design Code OB001 46T GLW Open Wagon – Lot 3909 and Lot 3930 Wagons

110001 to 110500 – Built to Lot 3909 by Ashford Works, October 1977 to April 1979.
110501 to 110800 – Built to Lot 3930 by Shildon Works, December 1978 to September 1979.
Design Codes: OB001B (Lot 3909) and OB001C (Lot 3930); Length over headstocks: 33ft 6in; Wheelbase: 20ft 9in; Springs: Long Link; 3ft 1½in diameter wheels; Air disc brakes and hand lever; 1ft 8½in Oleo Pneumatic Buffers; Roller bearings; Screw couplings; TOPS Code: OBA; double-arrow/Railfreight symbol carried.

These wagons differed between the lengths of the side drop door panels from the prototype 110000. The springs were later changed to the Brueninghaus design; Lot 3930 vehicles had them from new, but the code was unchanged from OBA.

ABOVE No. 110492, taken at South Lambeth goods yard, Battersea, in July 1980, is a Lot 3909 46T GLW open wagon in original condition and loaded with wire coils. It is in maroon livery with OBA code and double-arrow/Railfreight symbol. *Author's photo ref. W9049/DL*

LEFT No. 110146, taken at Hoo Junction Yard on 11 April 1982, is a Lot 3909 46T GLW open wagon in original condition and loaded with concrete sleepers. It is in maroon livery with OBA code and double-arrow/Railfreight symbol. *Author's photo ref. W11451/DL*

LEFT No. 110258, taken at Hoo Junction Yard on 1 August 1982, is a Lot 3909 46T GLW open wagon in original condition and loaded with black naval buoys. It is in maroon livery with OBA code and double-arrow/Railfreight symbol. *Author's photo ref. W11603/DL*

ABOVE No. 110238, taken at Rochester goods yard on 4 April 1982, is a Lot 3909 46T GLW open wagon in original condition but now fitted with Bruninghaus springs. It is in maroon livery with OBA code and double-arrow/Railfreight symbol. *Author's photo ref. W11389/DL*

CENTRE RIGHT This unidentified wagon, taken at Factory Junction, Battersea, in April 1978, is a Lot 3909 46T GLW open wagon in original condition and completely sheeted. It is in maroon livery with OBA code and double-arrow/Railfreight symbol. *Author's photo ref. W7658/DL*

RIGHT No. 110191, taken at St Blazey in August 1981, is a Lot 3909 46T GLW open wagon in original condition and now fitted with Brueninghaus springs. It is in maroon livery with OBA code and double-arrow/Railfreight symbol. *Author's photo ref. W9045/DL*

Design Code OB001 46T GLW Open Wagon – Lot 3930 Wagons

No. 110567, taken at South Lambeth goods yard, Battersea, in July 1980, is a Lot 3930 46T GLW open wagon in original condition and loaded with wire coils. It is in maroon livery with OBA code and double-arrow/Railfreight symbol. *Author's photo ref. W9051/DL*

No. 110588, taken at Hoo Junction Yard on 1 August 1982, is a Lot 3909 46T GLW open wagon in original condition and loaded with black naval buoys. It is in maroon livery with OBA code and double-arrow/Railfreight symbol. *Author's photo ref. W11602/DL*

No. 110621, taken at South Lambeth goods yard, Battersea, in April 1980, is a Lot 3930 46T GLW Open wagon in original condition and sheeted with grey plastic sheet. It is in maroon livery with OBA code and double-arrow/Railfreight symbol. *Author's photo ref. W9054/DL*

No. 110681, taken at South Lambeth goods yard, Battersea, in April 1980, is a Lot 3930 46T GLW open wagon in original condition and sheeted with grey plastic sheet. It is in maroon livery with OBA code and double-arrow/Railfreight symbol. *Author's photo ref. W9057/DL*

No. 110733, taken at Chichester goods yard on 1 February 1989, is a Lot 3930 46T GLW open wagon in original condition and with dividers in raised position. It is in maroon livery with OBA code and Railfreight symbol on flame red patch. *Author's photo ref. W14899/DL*

No. 110741, taken at Bury St. Edmunds goods yard on 11 March 1984, is a Lot 3930 46T GLW open wagon in original condition. It is in maroon livery with OBA code and double-arrow/Railfreight symbol. *Author's photo ref. W13726/DL*

No. 110635, taken at Plumstead goods yard on 11 December 1988, is a Lot 3930 46T GLW open wagon in original condition and loaded with logs. It is in flame red/grey livery with OBA code and double-arrow/Railfreight symbol. *Author's photo ref. W14347/DL*

ABOVE No. 110724, taken at Chichester goods yard on 1 February 1989, is a Lot 3930 46T GLW open wagon in original condition and with dividers in raised position. It is in flame red/grey livery with OBA code and double-arrow/Railfreight symbol. *Author's photo ref. W14897/DL*

CENTRE RIGHT No. 110637, taken at Dumfries goods yard on 25 October 1988, is a Lot 3930 46T GLW open wagon in original condition. It is in flame red/grey livery with OBA code and double-arrow/Railfreight symbol. *Author's photo ref. W14214/DL*

RIGHT No. 110724, taken at Plumstead goods yard on 11 December 1988, is a Lot 3930 46T GLW open wagon in original condition and loaded with logs. It is in flame red/grey livery with OBA code and double-arrow/Railfreight symbol. *Author's photo ref. W14350/DL*

Design Code OB001 46T GLW Open Wagon – Lot 3909 and Lot 3930 Wagons (CCE transfers as ZDA BASS)

Virtually the whole of the Lot 3909 wagons were transferred to departmental stock and the CCE had most of them. All were coded ZDA BASS and all, including the small number from Lot 3930, had Brueninghaus springs. Known numbers are as follows:

DC110001-4/8-15/7-35/7-45/7-63/5-99; DC110100-18/20-31/3-47/9-56/8-93/5-9; DC110200-2/4-32/4-6-49/51-6/8-62/4-7/9-99; DC110300/2-11/5-22/4-31/3-9/41-7/9/50/2-61/5/6/8/70/2-91/4/5/7-9; DC110400-3/5-9/11-4/7-24/6-31/3-5/7/40/2/4/5/7/9/51/3-65/7-71/3-5/7-82/5; DC110584/6; DC110617/61/9/84; DC110708/80/2

ABOVE No. DC110001, taken at Hither Green PAD on 19 March 1989, is a Design Code OB001C OBA 46T GLW open wagon with Brueninghaus springs and transferred to the CCE. It is in maroon livery with white lettering, ZDA code and double-arrow/Railfreight symbol. *Author's photo ref. W15921/DL*

CENTRE LEFT No. DC110428, taken at Southampton Northam goods yard on 10 March 1989, is a Design Code OB001C OBA 46T GLW open wagon with Brueninghaus springs and transferred to the CCE. It is in yellow/grey livery with white lettering, ZDA code and BASS name in black. *Author's photo ref. W15507/DL*

LEFT No. DC110334, taken at Hoo Junction Yard in November 1988, is a Design Code OB001C OBA 46T GLW open wagon with Brueninghaus springs and transferred to the CCE. It is in yellow/grey livery with white lettering, ZDA code and BASS name in black. *Author's photo ref. W14775/DL*

No. DC110677, taken at Peterborough Yard on 30 May 1992, is a Design Code OB001C OBA 46T GLW open wagon transferred to the CCE and rebuilt as a ZCA SEA URCHIN. It is in yellow/grey livery with white lettering and ZCA code in black and SEA URCHIN name in black. *Author's photo ref. W16957/DL*

Design Code OB001 46T GLW Open Wagon – CCE transfers as ZDA BASS converted to SEA URCHIN

A number of the transferred ZDA BASS wagons were given new bodywork with fixed sides and ends of low height. Known numbers are as follows:

DC110257; DC110389; DC110619/30/77; DC110728

Design Code OB001 46T GLW Open Wagon – Lot 3909 and Lot 3930 Wagons (CS&TE transfers)

The CS&TE also received transferred OBAs, all with Brueninghaus springs. Known numbers are as follows:

KDC110005-7/16/36/46/64; KDC110119/32/48/57/94; KDC110203/35/50/63/8; KDC110301/12-4/23/32/40/8/51/62-4/7/9/71/96; KDC110404/10/5/6 /25/32/6/8/9/41/3/8/50/2/66/72/83; KDC110579/88; KDC110612/36/89

Other transferred OBAs went to the CM&EE. Known numbers are as follows:

ADC110233/57; ADC110392/3; ADC110446/76; ADC110515/6/8-28; ADC110630/53

No. KDC110588, taken at Woking Yard on 31 March 1992, is a Design Code OB001C OBA 46T GLW open wagon transferred to the S&TE as a ZDA. It is in yellow/flame red livery with white lettering and ZCA code on black and SAT-LINK name in black. *Author's photo ref. W16673/DL*

Design Code OB001 46T GLW Open Wagon – Lot 3930 Wagons converted to RR046A Runner wagons

These conversions all came from Lot 3930. Known numbers are as follows:

110532/8/40/2/53/67/70/2/6, 110601-3/13/22/32/4/40/75/9/95/8/9, 110707/9/17/35/6/42/4/5/7/9/51/64/74/6/85/9/96

No. 110542, taken at BSC Shelton Steelworks, Etruria, Stoke-on-Trent, on 7 June 1992, is a Design Code OB001C OBA 46T GLW open wagon converted to an RRA runner wagon. It is in light grey livery with white lettering on black, RRA code and DO NOT LOAD lettering. *Author's photo ref. W17082/DL*

No. 110570, taken at Cardiff Tidal Sidings Yard on 6 June 1992, is a Design Code OB001C OBA 46T GLW open wagon converted to an RRA runner wagon. It is in freight brown livery with white lettering and RRA code. *Author's photo ref. W17070/DL*

No. 110602, taken at Middlesbrough goods yard on 13 June 1992, is a Design Code OB001C OBA 46T GLW open wagon converted to an RRA runner wagon. It is in light grey livery with white lettering on black, RRA code and DO NOT LOAD lettering. *Author's photo ref. W17093/DL*

No. 110584, taken at Biggleswade Plasmor depot on 20 February 1989, is a Design Code OB001C OBA 46T GLW open wagon converted to a high-end OBA for Plasmor traffic. It is in green/white band/orange livery with white OBA code, [logo] PLASMOR BLOCKFREIGHT lettering and double-arrow symbols. *Author's photo ref. W15106/DL*

Design Code OB001 46T GLW Open Wagon – Lot 3930 Wagons converted to OB001E for PLASMOR traffic

These conversions all came from Lot 3930 and worked from Heck, near Selby, to Biggleswade, Bow and Wymondham with breeze blocks. Known numbers are as follows:

110531/5/7/41/3/5/50/62/8/78/82/4/6/7/98; 110604/8/9/11/4/5/8/21/5/6/9/33/42/7/51/2/4/7/60/2/3/5/6/85; 110703/18/9/25/30/7/46/54/60/3/77/95

One wagon, 110793, was converted to an OTA timber wagon.

No. 110754, taken at Biggleswade Plasmor depot on 20 February 1989, is a Design Code OB001C OBA 46T GLW open wagon converted to a high-end OBA for Plasmor traffic. It is in weathered maroon livery with white Railfreight lettering. *Author's photo ref. W15108/DL*

No. 110666, taken at Peterborough Yard on 30 May 1992, is a Design Code OB001C OBA 46T GLW open wagon converted to a high-end OBA for Plasmor traffic. It is in recently-repainted green/white band/orange livery with black OBA code. *Author's photo ref. W16971/DL*

9
Design Code OC001
OCA 46T Open Goods Wagon

112000 to 112399 – Built to Lot 4014 by Shildon Works, October 1981 to March 1982; Design Code: OC001A; Length over headstocks: 33ft 6in; Wheelbase: 20ft 9in; Springs: Brueninghaus; 3ft 1½in diameter wheels; Air disc brakes and hand lever; 1ft 8½in Oleo Pneumatic Buffers; Roller bearings; Screw couplings; TOPS Code: OCA; double-arrow/Railfreight symbol carried.

These wagons were essentially a taller version of the production SPA design (see Chapter 11). A number were transferred to the CCE as ZDA BASS wagons and some of these were rebuilt to ZCA SEAHORSE wagons. Others were converted to OTA timber wagons in a number of forms.

No. 112147, taken at Goole yard on 2 October 1982, is a Design Code OC001A OBA 46T GLW open wagon in original condition. It is in flame red livery with white lettering, OCA code and double-arrow/Railfreight symbol. *Author's photo ref. W12115/DL*

No. 112252, taken at Hoo Junction Yard on 14 March 1982, is a Design Code OC001A 46T GLW open wagon in original condition and loaded with wire coils. It is in flame red livery with OCA code and double-arrow/Railfreight symbol. *Author's photo ref. W11312/DL*

No. 112159, taken at Northwich yard on 3 October 1982, is a Design Code OC001A 46T GLW open wagon in original condition. It is in flame red livery with OCA code and double-arrow/Railfreight symbol. *Author's photo ref. W12259/DL*

No. 112348, taken at Toton Yard on 20 February 1983, is a Design Code OC001A 46T GLW open wagon in original condition and sheeted with grey plastic sheets. It is in flame red livery. *Author's photo ref. W12649/DL*

This unidentified wagon, taken at Newark goods yard on 19 February 1983, is a Design Code OC001A 46T GLW open wagon in original condition with sides lowered. It is in flame red livery. *Author's photo ref. W12540/DL*

No. 112230, taken at Carlisle Currock C&W depot on 16 June 1992, is a Design Code OC001A 46T GLW open wagon in original condition. It is in Sector dark grey/yellow livery with OCA code, RfD symbol and lettered 'TO WORK BETWEEN CARLISLE CURROCK 09191 AND ST BLAZEY 85221'. *Author's photo ref. W17171/DL*

No. 112244, taken at Cardiff Tidal Yard on 6 June 1992, is a Design Code OC001A 46T GLW open wagon in original condition and loaded with wagon wheels. It is in Sector dark grey/yellow livery with OCA code, RfD symbol and lettered 'RETURN TO CURROCK 09191'. *Author's photo ref. W17076/DL*

Design Code OC001A 46T GLW Open Wagons – Wagons transferred to the CCE as ZDA BASS

A large proportion of the early wagons of this type were transferred to the CCE as ZDA BASS (Design Code ZD148B). Known numbers are as follows:

DC112000/3/20/1/6-8/30-7/41/3-9/51-8/60-2/5/6/9/71/2/4/5/7/9/81/3/5-93/6/7/9; 112101/3-7/9/11/2/4-6/8-28/30/1/3-9/41/4-6/8/50/2/3/5/6/8; 112273, 112380

LEFT No. DC112273, taken at Hoo Junction Yard on 5 May 1989, is a Design Code OC001A 46T GLW open wagon in original condition and transferred to the CCE. It is in yellow/grey livery with ZDA code and BASS name in black. *Author's photo ref. W16125/DL*

No. DC112080, taken at Whitemoor Yard, March, on 11 March 1984, is a Design Code OC001A 46T GLW open wagon in original condition and transferred to the CCE. It retains flame red livery with ZDA Code and white BASS name on yellow patch. *Author's photo ref. W13772/DL*

No. DC112273, taken at Hither Green PAD on 12 April 1992, is a Design Code OC001A 46T GLW open wagon in original condition and transferred to the CCE. It is in Sector dark grey/yellow livery with ZDA code and RfD symbol but no FISHKND name. *Author's photo ref. W16812/DL*

Design Code OC001A 46T GLW Open Wagons – Wagons transferred to the CCE converted to ZCA SEAHORSE

DC112029/39/40/2/50/9/64/8/70/3/6/8/80/2/4/94/5/8; 112100/2/8/10/3/32/40/2/3/7/9/51/4/7

Many of the ZDA BASS wagons were recoded ZCA SEAHORSE (Design Code ZC515A). Known numbers are as follows:

Initially, these wagons operated with the doors fixed closed, as seen above, but subsequently received low-height sides while retaining the original ends.

No. DC112039, taken at Hoo Junction Yard on 7 December 1988, is a Design Code OC001A 46T GLW open wagon in original condition and transferred to the CCE with doors fixed. It is in yellow/grey livery with ZCA code in white and SEAHORSE name in black. *Author's photo ref. W14497/DL*

No. DC112094, taken at Hoo Junction Yard on 1 July 1989, is a Design Code OC001A 46T GLW open wagon converted to a ZCA SEAHORSE. It is in yellow/grey livery with ZCA code in white and SEAHORSE name in black. *Author's photo ref. W16333/DL*

Speedlink

No. DC112082, taken at Hoo Junction Yard on 1 July 1989, is a Design Code OC001A 46T GLW open wagon converted to a ZCA SEAHORSE. It is in yellow/grey livery with ZCA code in white and SEAHORSE name in black. *Author's photo ref. W16337/DL*

No. DC112039, taken at Hoo Junction Yard on 1 July 1989, is a Design Code OC001A 46T GLW open wagon converted to a ZCA SEAHORSE. It is in yellow/grey livery with ZCA code in white and SEAHORSE name in black. *Author's photo ref. W16347/DL*

Wagons transferred to the CM&EE

These vehicles were transferred to the CM&EE and, as far as is known, remained unaltered. Known numbers are as follows:

ADC112001/2/4-19/22-5

Design Code OC001A 46T GLW Open Wagons – Wagons converted to OTA Timber wagons

Certain wagons were converted to OTA timber wagons, as seen above, but fully accurate details seem uncertain. Known numbers for OT001A are as follows:

112067; 112160-2/6/7/70/5/8/80/2/3/5-8/91/4/6; 112207/8/ 10/2/6/22/5/31/4-7/9/41/3/48/51/3/5/7/63/6/8/72/5/8/80/1/3/ 8-91/9; 112302/3/8/10/6-9/23/4/7/9/30/2-4/6/8-40/2/5/7/9/ 51/2/5/64-6/9/70/2/6/8/81-3/7-9/91/6/9

No. 112324, taken at Cardiff Tidal Sidings Yard on 6 June 1992, is a Design Code OC001A 46T GLW open wagon converted to an OTA Timber wagon. It retains flame red livery with OTA code. *Author's photo ref. W17062/DL*

Some have extended ends, as seen above, but others have a shaped end. Known to have the squared ends are 112185, 112225 and 112324/47.

There was a second variant of OTA which appears to have been dedicated to, and in the livery of, Thames Board Ltd. Known numbers for OT001C are as follows:

112184/9/90; 112204/20/6/64/7/71/82/6/94; 112301/4/12/3/22/38/41/53/71/80/4-6

Finally, there was a single example of Design Code OT001B which cannot be illustrated. The number was as follows:

112292

No. 112312, taken at Workington goods yard on 25 October 1988, is a Design Code OC001A 46T GLW open wagon converted to an OTA timber wagon. It is in blue/white livery with OTA code and THAMES BOARD LTD lettering. *Author's photo ref. W14194/DL*

No. 112225, taken at Warrington Arpley Yard on 23 October 1988, is a Design Code OC001A 46T GLW open wagon converted to an OTA timber wagon and loaded with pine logs from Scotland. It retains flame red livery with OTA code. *Author's photo ref. W14161/DL*

No. 112364, taken at Southampton Northam goods yard on 1 February 1989, is a Design Code OC001A 46T GLW open wagon converted to an OTA timber wagon and loaded with pine logs from Scotland. It retains flame red livery with OTA code. *Author's photo ref. W14945/DL*

No. 112268, taken at Cardiff Tidal Sidings Yard on 6 June 1992, is a Design Code OC001A 46T GLW open wagon converted to an OTA timber wagon for Shotton Paper. It is in light green/white livery with OTA code. *Author's photo ref. W17063/DL*

No. 112182, taken at Inverness goods yard on 16 June 1992, is a Design Code OC001A 46T GLW open wagon converted to an OTA timber wagon for Shotton Paper. It is in light green/white livery with OTA code. *Author's photo ref. W17153/DL*

10
Design Code OD001
ODA 12T Pipe Wagon

113000 to 113049 – Converted to Lot 4030 by Shildon Works, 1983; Design Codes: OD001A; Length over headstocks: 21ft 6in; Wheelbase: 12ft 0in; Springs: Brueninghaus; 3ft 1½in diameter wheels; Air disc brakes and hand lever with shoes; Change-over Lever; 1ft 7in Oleo Pneumatic Buffers; Roller bearings; Screw couplings; TOPS Code: ODA; double-arrow/Railfreight symbol carried.

These wagons were conversions of vacuum-braked 12T pipe wagons from Lot 3335, Diagram 1/462, and were probably produced to serve the needs of the Ministry of Defence in the same manner as the VEAs (see Chapter 13). Allocated 466000 to 466049 in the 'steel' number range, this was changed to numbers in the 'open' range.

No. 113013, taken at Severn Tunnel Junction Yard on 19 November 1983, is a Design Code OD001A 12T pipe wagon. It is in flame red/grey livery with white lettering, ODA code and double-arrow/Railfreight symbol. *Author's photo ref. W13533/DL*

The following list gives the former identities of the ODA wagons:

113000 (B741855); 113001 (B741792); 113002 (B741847); 113003 (B741785); 113004 (B741872); 113005 (B741841); 113006 (B741857); 113007 (B741874); 113008 (B741878); 113009 (B741773); 113010 (B741859); 113011 (B741933); 113012 (B741879); 113013 (B741818); 113014 (B741760); 113015 (B741905); 113016 (B741849); 113017 (B741830); 113018 (B741788); 113019 (B741936); 113020 (B741875); 113021 (B741757); 113022 (B741899); 113023 (B741798); 113024 (B741754); 113025 (B741931); 113026 (B741777); 113027 (B741853); 113028 (B741865); 113029 (B741843); 113030 (B741916); 113031 (B741891); 113032 (B741911); 113033 (B741906); 113034 (B741892); 113035 (B741817); 113036 (B741882), 113037 (B741888), 113038 (B741912), 113039 (B741942), 113040 (B741928), 113041 (B741900); 113042 (B741816); 113043 (B741885); 113044 (B741825); 113045 (B741850); 113046 (B741766); 113047 (B741828); 113048 (B741927); 113049 (B741763)

ABOVE No. 113023, taken at Shildon Works on 16 April 1983, is a brand-new Design Code OD001A 12T pipe wagon. It is in flame red/grey livery with white lettering, ODA code and double-arrow/Railfreight symbol. *Author's photo ref. W4982/DL*

Nos. 113036 (above) and 113048 (below), taken at Dinton goods yard on 10 June 1983, are Design Code OD001A 12T pipe wagons in as-new condition. They are in flame red/grey livery with white lettering, ODA code and double-arrow/Railfreight symbol. *Author's photo ref. W13086/DL/Author's photo ref. W13084/DL*

11
Design Code SP020A
SPA 46T Plate Wagon

460000 to 460001 – Converted to Lot 3914 by Ashford Works, May 1977; Design Code: SP019A; Length over headstocks: 33ft 6in; Wheelbase: 20ft 9in; Springs: Long Link; 3ft ½in diameter wheels; Air disc brakes and hand lever; 1ft 8½in Oleo Pneumatic Buffers; Roller bearings; Screw couplings; TOPS Code: SPA; double-arrow/Railfreight symbol carried.

These wagons were conversions of STEEL ABs 400100 and 400142 (see Volume 1 of this series) and had all-steel low-height bodywork with four-part drop sides. 460000 became DC460000, a ZXQ structure gauging car, and 460001 became an RRA runner wagon, presumably with bodywork removed. 460502 to 460601 were originally part of the STEEL AB batch, Lot 3728, but they were never converted and the numbers reallocated.

No. 460000, taken at Maidstone West goods yard in September 1977 in an exhibition train, is a Design Code SP019A SPA 46T GLW plate wagon in original condition. It is in maroon livery with white lettering, SPA code and double-arrow/Railfreight symbol. *Author's photo ref. W7756/DL*

Design Code SP020A 46T Plate Wagon

460002 to 460601 – Built to Lot 3839 by Shildon Works, June 1979 to February 1980.
460602 to 461101 – Built to Lot 3962 by Shildon Works, May 1980 to February 1981.
Design Code: SP020A; Length over headstocks: 33ft 6in; Wheelbase: 20ft 9in; Springs: Brueninghaus; 3ft 1½in diameter wheels; Air disc brakes and hand lever; 1ft 8½in Oleo Pneumatic Buffers; Roller bearings; Screw couplings; TOPS Code: SPA; double-arrow/Railfreight symbol carried.

No. 460002, taken at Cardiff Tidal Sidings Yard on 11 September 1982, is a Design Code SP020A SPA 46T GLW plate wagon in original condition. It is in flame red livery with white lettering, SPA code and double-arrow/Railfreight symbol. *Author's photo ref. W11770/DL*

These wagons were the production batch of the SPA and differed by having three-part drop sides and Brueninghaus springs. 461102 to 461501 were planned under Lot 3962 and 461502 to 461601 were planned under Lot 3995 but both batches were cancelled. Many wagons were transferred to the CCE as ZAA PIKE. Others were converted to more specialised steel-carrying wagons.

No. 460404, taken at Rotherham steel terminal on 22 December 1988, is a Design Code SP020A SPA 46T GLW plate wagon in original condition. It is in flame red livery with white lettering, SPA code and double-arrow/Railfreight symbol. *Author's photo ref. W14115/DL*

ABOVE No. 460870, taken at Rochester goods yard on 5 May 1984, is a Design Code SP020A SPA 46T GLW plate wagon in original condition and with load sheeted with grey plastic sheets. It is in flame red livery with white lettering, SPA code and double-arrow/Railfreight symbol. *Author's photo ref. W13893/DL*

CENTRE RIGHT No. 460902, taken at Toton Yard on 20 February 1983, is a Design Code SP020A SPA 46T GLW plate wagon in original condition and with a load of army trailers. It is in flame red livery with white lettering, SPA code and double-arrow/Railfreight symbol. *Author's photo ref. W12620/DL*

RIGHT No. 460339, taken at Cardiff Rod Mill Yard on 6 June 1992, is a Design Code SP020A SPA 46T GLW plate wagon in original condition and with wire coil load. It is in flame red livery with white lettering, SPA code and double-arrow/Railfreight symbol. *Author's photo ref. W17046/DL*

No. 460330, taken at Hoo Junction Yard in October 1981, is a Design Code SP020A SPA 46T GLW plate wagon in original condition and with industrial load. It is in flame red livery with white lettering, SPA code and double-arrow/Railfreight symbol. *Author's photo ref. W9070/DL*

No. 460752, taken at Strood goods yard on 8 March 1983, is a Design Code SP020A SPA 46T GLW plate wagon in original condition and with a load of smokeless fuel. It is in flame red livery with white lettering, SPA code and double-arrow/Railfreight symbol. *Author's photo ref. W12704/DL*

Design Code SP020A 46T Plate Wagon – Wagons transferred to the CCE as ZAA PIKE

A large proportion of the wagons of this type were transferred to the CCE as ZAA PIKE (Design Code ZA008A). Known numbers are as follows:

DC460003/5-8/11-7/9/20/2-35/7-9/41-52/5-60/3/5-7/9/71-81/3-5/7-92/4-8; DC460100 /1/3-7/9-11/3-7/21/4-6/8-33/5/6/8-43/5-7/9/51/4-7/9/60/2-74/6-8/80/2-5/7/9/91-9; 460200-6/8/9/14/5/7/9/20/2/3/5/6/8/31-9/41-3/5-50/2-65/7/71-4/6-9/81/2/4-93/5-7; DC460300-6/8/9/11-4/7/8/21-9/31/45; DC460400/7/14/9/45/90; DC460518/39/50/71; DC460655/7/65; DC460750/1/95; DC460820/61/83; DC460935/9/49; DC461082/96/9

Some of the wagons of this type were later converted to ZCA SEAHARE (Design Code ZC010A), details being found on page 122.

ABOVE No. DC460029, taken at Southampton Northam goods yard on 10 March 1989, is a Design Code SP020A SPA 46T GLW plate wagon in original condition after transfer to the CCE and with a load of chaired sleepers. It is in weathered flame red livery with white lettering, ZAA code, Railfreight symbol and faded PIKE name. *Author's photo ref. W15503/DL*

No. DC460018 (above), loaded with withdrawn No. DW84999, and No. DC460094 (right), loaded with withdrawn No. DW84998, taken at Hoo Junction Yard on 20 September 1989, are Design Code SP020A plate wagons transferred to the CCE and carrying the two withdrawn portions of the black-liveried girder wagon set. Livery is yellow/grey with ZAA code and PIKE name in black. *Author's photo ref. W16504/DL/Author's photo ref. W16505/DL*

These wagons were ZAA PIKEs with side doors sealed for ballast and spoil and recoded ZCA SEAHARE (Design Code ZC010A). Known numbers are as follows:

DC460002/4/9/10/8/21/36/40/53/4/61/2/4/8/70/82/6/93/9; DC460102/8/12/22/34/44/8/52/3/8/61/75/9/86/8/90; DC460207/10/2/3/6/8/24/7/9/30/40/4/51/68-70/5/80/3/94/8/9; DC460307/10/5/6/9/20/30/63; DC460472; DC460529

No. DC460032, taken at Peterborough Yard on 26 February 1989, is a Design Code SP020A SPA 46T GLW plate wagon in original condition after transfer to the CCE and with a load of PW machinery. It is in yellow/grey livery with white lettering, ZAA code and PIKE name in black. *Author's photo ref. W15406/DL*

No. DC460094, taken at Hitchin Yard on 30 May 1992, is a Design Code SP020A SPA 46T GLW plate wagon in original condition after transfer to the CCE. It is in yellow/grey livery with white lettering, ZAA code, PIKE name in black and CIVILINK in grey. *Author's photo ref. W16949/DL*

No. DC460054, taken at Hoo Junction Yard on 4 June 1992, is a Design Code SP020A SPA 46T GLW plate wagon in original condition after transfer to the CCE and with side doors sealed. It is in yellow/grey livery with white lettering, ZCA code, SEAHARE name in black and SIDE DOORS SEALED in white on a black panel. *Author's photo ref. W17040/DL*

No. 460822, taken at Rotherham steel terminal on 22 October 1988, is a Design Code SP020A SPA 46T GLW plate wagon after conversion to an SDA double bolster and with a load of steel plate. It is in weathered flame red livery with white lettering and SDA code. *Author's photo ref. W14113/DL*

Design Code SP020A 46T Plate Wagon – Wagons converted to SDA (Design Code SD001A)

These wagons were converted to Double Bolster type with the sides removed and three bolsters fitted. Known numbers are as follows:

460612/3/26/7/74/83; 460706/9/18/23/54/71/5; 460813/21/2/5/6/56/79/89; 460906/16/20/73; 461000/28/58/76

Design Code SP020A 46T Plate Wagon – Wagons converted to SEA (Design Code SE002A)

These wagons were given a permanent telescopic hood. Known numbers are as follows:

460385; 460454; 460514/46/83; 460608/19/70/8/97; 460724/44/60/73/9/83/93; 460816/32/65/72/96; 460904/17/41/52/66/83/6/9/92; 461005/12/57; 461100

No. 460608, taken at Cardiff Rod Mill Sidings on 6 June 1992, is a Design Code SP020A SPA 46T GLW plate wagon after conversion to an SEA rod coil wagon. It is in weathered flame red livery with white lettering, SEA code, double-arrow/Railfreight symbol, blue permanent sheet with Railfreight Metals symbol and name plus ASW symbol and lettered Cardiff Rod Mill Quality rods from Wales. *Author's photo ref. W17048/DL*

No. 461066, taken at Whitemoor Yard, March, on 11 March 1984, is a Design Code SP020A SPA 46T GLW plate wagon after conversion to an SHA (KTA) coil wagon. It is in weathered flame red livery with white lettering, SHA code and double-arrow/Railfreight symbol. *Author's photo ref. W13776/DL*

Design Code SP020A 46T Plate Wagon – Wagons converted to SHA, formerly KTA (Design Code SH002A)

These wagons were given floor spigots to carry three strip coil rolls 'eye-to-sky', which were normally sheeted. Known numbers are as follows:

460390; 460492; 460522/42;
460707/22/6/9/53/8/61/81/92/9; 460811/42/7/98;
460924/31/43/51/68/76/84/5/94; 461010/37/8/55/66

Design Code SP020A 46T Plate Wagon – Wagons converted to SKA, formerly KOA (Design Code SK003A)

These wagons had the sides removed and replaced with supporting bars and with longitudinal floor rails and vertical end posts. Known numbers are as follows:

460362/82; 460416/21/9-31/41/8/63/4/82/6;
460517/9/61/7/72/5/92; 460601/14/21/59/66/79/85/8;
460700/12/28/43/66/96; 460809/46/9/50; 460909/53;
461004/11/47/52/6/68/79/84/5/93

No. 460743, taken at Warrington Arpley Yard on 13 August 1983, is a Design Code SP020A SPA 46T GLW plate wagon after conversion to an SKA (KOA) wire coil wagon. It is in weathered flame red livery with white lettering and KOA code. *Author's photo ref. W13280/DL*

12
Design Code VD001 VDA 40T Vanfit

200650 to 200979 – Built to Lot 3855 by Ashford Works, January 1976 to November 1976.

210100 to 210399 – Built to Lot 3908 by Shildon Works, August 1977 to November 1978.

Design Codes: VD001A; Length over headstocks: 33ft 6in; Wheelbase: 20ft 9in; Springs: Friction Link; 3ft 1½in diameter wheels; Air disc brakes and hand lever; 1ft 8½in Oleo Pneumatic Buffers; Roller bearings; Screw couplings; TOPS Code: VDA; double-arrow/Railfreight symbol carried.

Certain vans from this batch were in the Rowntree's livery (see page 128). Others were converted to OTA timber wagons (see page 131) and RRA Runner wagons (see page 135).

No. 200658, taken at Factory Junction, Battersea, on 26 August 1978, is a Design Code VD001A VDA 40T GLW open wagon in original condition. It is in maroon livery with white lettering, OBA code and double-arrow/Railfreight symbol. *Author's photo ref. W6841/DL*

No. 200760, taken at Briton Ferry Yard in April 1976, is a Design Code VD001A 40T GLW van in brand-new condition. It is in maroon livery with VDA code and double-arrow symbol and Railfreight lettering. *Author's photo ref. W5597/DL*

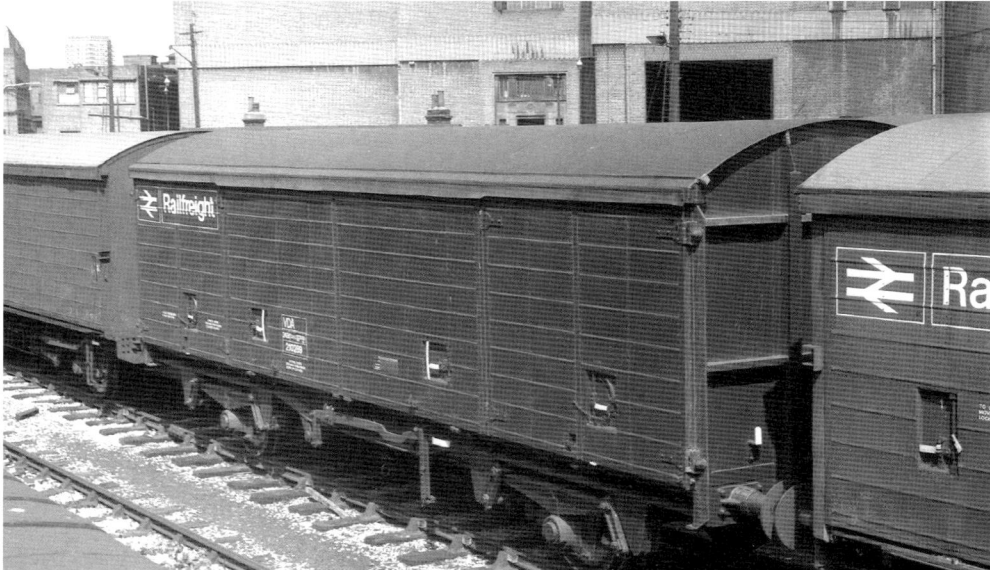

No. 210289, taken at South Lambeth goods yard, Battersea, on 24 August 1978, is a Design Code VD001A 40T GLW van in brand-new condition. It is in maroon livery with VDA code and double-arrow symbol and Railfreight lettering. *Author's photo ref. W6835/DL*

No. 200860, taken at Dagenham Yard on 1 May 1982, is a Design Code VD001A 40T GLW van in original condition. It is in flame red/grey livery with VDA code and double-arrow symbol and Railfreight lettering. *Author's photo ref. W11477/DL*

No. 200688, taken at Cardiff Radyr Yard on 19 November 1983, is a Design Code VD001A 40T GLW van in original condition. It is in flame red/grey livery with VDA code and double-arrow symbol and Railfreight lettering. *Author's photo ref. W13564/DL*

No. 200723, taken at Basingstoke Yard on 31 March 1992, is a Design Code VD001A 40T GLW van in original condition. It is in Sector dark grey/yellow livery with VDA code and RfD symbol. *Author's photo ref. W16667/DL*

No. 210374, taken at Doncaster Belmont Yard on 31 May 1992, is a Design Code VD001A 40T GLW van in original condition. It is in Sector dark grey/yellow livery with VDA code and RfD symbol. *Author's photo ref. W17005/DL*

No. 200999, taken at Dover Yard in June 1981, is a Design Code VD001B VDA 40T GLW van in original condition. It is in maroon livery with white roof, white lettering, VDA code and double-arrow/Railfreight symbol. *Author's photo ref. W9019/DL*

Design Code VD001 40T Vanfit – Lot 3890 and Rowntree's vans

200980 to 200999 – Built to Lot 3890 by Ashford Works, September 1976 to November 1976; Design Code: VD001A; Length over headstocks: 33ft 6in; Wheelbase: 20ft 9in; Springs: Friction Link; 3ft 1½in diameter wheels; Air shoe brakes and hand lever; 1ft 8½in Oleo Pneumatic Buffers; Roller bearings; Screw couplings; TOPS Code: VDA; double-arrow/Railfreight symbol carried.

This small batch is believed to have been given insulated roofs for Rowntree's chocolate traffic, having white roofs to identify them.

Other vans from Design Code VD001A were converted, together with 12 VBBs (see Volume 1, Chapter 10 for full details of this type) and others from Design Code VD001C (see page 130). Known numbers were:

200250/1/74/5/87/8/94-9 (VBBs): 200650/80/1; 200702/3/6/ 13/6/25/45/52/5/60/3/8 /73/9/80/6/9/91-7, 200800-3/20/1/3/44/61/7/9/91/2; 200929/36/44/53/64-6/77; 210144-6/52/3/61/95/8; 210211/6/9/35/49/53/61/3/9/77/80/ 6/93; 210301-20/3-8/32

200987 was delivered in an all-white livery in error and, as far as is known, was never painted in any other livery. It had been withdrawn by 1990.

The Rowntree's traffic was lost to rail in 1987 and the vans allocated to Pool 4783 were dispersed.

Of the original Lot 3890 batch, four became OTA timber wagons (see page 132 for 200982, others were 200980/1/5). The others were transferred to the CE and S&T, with another four meeting early withdrawal (200990/3/8/9).

No. 200987, taken at Dover Yard in June 1981, is a Design Code VD001B VDA 41T GLW van in original condition. It is in weathered white livery with white roof, black lettering and VDA code. *Author's photo ref. W9018/DL*

No. 200745, taken at Dover Yard in June 1981, is a Design Code VD001A VDA 41T GLW van with insulated roof. It is in maroon livery with white roof, white lettering, VDA code and double-arrow/Railfreight symbol. *Author's photo ref. W9014/DL*

No. 201025, taken at Nunhead in July 1978, is a Design Code VD001C VDA 41T GLW van with insulated roof. It is in maroon livery with white roof, white lettering, VDA code and double-arrow/Railfreight symbol. *Author's photo ref. W7098/DL*

No. 200791, taken at York Dringhouses Yard on 26 November 1983, is a Design Code VD001A VDA 40T GLW van with insulated roof. It is in flame red/grey livery with white roof, white lettering, VDA code and double-arrow/Railfreight symbol. *Author's photo ref. W13703/DL*

No. 210319, taken at York Dringhouses Yard on 26 November 1983, is a Design Code VD001A VDA 41T GLW van with insulated roof. It is in maroon livery with white roof, white lettering, VDA code and double-arrow/Railfreight symbol. *Author's photo ref. W13704/DL*

No. 201026, taken at Nunhead in July 1977, is a Design Code VD001C VDA 40T GLW van in original condition. It is in maroon livery with white roof, white lettering, VDA code and double-arrow/Railfreight symbol. *Author's photo ref. W6813/DL*

Design Code VD001 40T Vanfit – Lot 3856

201000 to 201099 – Built to Lot 3856 by Shildon Works, November 1975 to March 1976; Design Code: VD001C; Length over headstocks: 33ft 6in; Wheelbase: 20ft 9in; Springs: Taperlite; 3ft 1½in diameter wheels; Air disc brakes and hand lever; 1ft 8½in Oleo Pneumatic Buffers; Roller bearings; Screw couplings; TOPS Code: VDA; double-arrow/Railfreight symbol carried.

This batch was deemed experimental and tested out the Taperlite form of suspension. Certain vans were given insulated white-painted roofs for the Rowntree's traffic. Known numbers were as follows:

201008/20/5/8/30/40/5/54/6/8/61/71/86/90/8

Other vans were converted to OTA timber wagons (see page 131), some passing to the CCE as sleeper wagons.

No. 201021, taken at Hoo Junction Yard in March 1981, is a Design Code VD001C 40T GLW van in original condition. It is in experimental flame red/white livery with VDA code in black and double-arrow/Railfreight symbol in white. *Author's photo ref. W9020/DL*

No. 201082, taken at Hoo Junction Yard on 11 January 1989, is a Design Code VD001C 40T GLW van in original condition. It is in faded flame red/grey livery with VDA code and double-arrow symbol and Railfreight lettering. *Author's photo ref. W14815/DL*

Design Code VD001 40T Vanfit – Vans converted to OTA Timber wagons

Certain vans were converted to OTA timber wagons with original ends retained and stanchions and straps fitted to the floor. Known numbers were as follows:

OT002A (Ex-VD001A): 200708/20/1/8/32/6/40/6/70/80, 200814/23/37/9/48/9/58/60/1/92, 200930/3/4/45/53/65/ 6/74, 210144/93, 210219, 210352/7/63
OT002B (Ex-VD001C): 201029/40/61/93
OT002C (Ex-VD001A): 200817/22
OT002D (Ex-VD001B): 200980-2/5
0T002E (Ex-Experimental): 201070
0T002F (Ex-VD001A): 200944

No. 200721, taken at Hoo Junction Yard on 15 March 1989, is a Design Code VD001A converted to a Design Code OT002A timber wagon. Livery is flame red/black with OTA code. *Author's photo ref. W15834/DL*

No. 200966, taken at Hoo Junction Yard on 15 March 1989, is a Design Code VD001A converted to a Design Code OT002A timber wagon. Livery is flame red/black with OTA code. *Author's photo ref. W15832/DL*

No. 201029, taken at Chichester goods yard on 1 February 1989, is a Design Code VD001C converted to a Design Code OT002B timber wagon. Livery is flame red/black with OTA code. *Author's photo ref. W14884/DL*

No. 200982, taken at Hexham goods yard on 28 October 1988, is a Design Code VD001B converted to a Design Code OT002D timber wagon. Livery is flame red/black with OTA code. *Author's photo ref. W14290/DL*

No. 200822, taken at Hexham goods yard on 28 October 1988, is a Design Code VD001A converted to a Design Code OT002D timber wagon. Livery is flame red/black with OTA code. *Author's photo ref. W14286/DL*

No. 200822, taken at Hoo Junction Yard on 1 July 1989 whilst being loaded, is a Design Code VD001A converted to a Design Code OT002D timber wagon. Livery is light blue/white/black with OTA code and KRONOSPAN lettering. *Author's photo ref. W16365/DL*

No. 201040, taken at Hoo Junction Yard on 1 June 1989 whilst being loaded, is a Design Code VD001C converted to a Design Code OT002B timber wagon. Livery is light blue/white/black with OTA code and KRONOSPAN lettering. *Author's photo ref. W16291/DL*

No. DC201093, taken at Woking goods yard on 31 March 1992, is a Design Code VD001C converted to a Design Code OT002B timber wagon and transferred to the CCE. Livery is light blue/white/black with ZRA code and KRONOSPAN lettering. *Author's photo ref. W16668B/DL*

No. DC201070, taken at Eastleigh Yard on 31 March 1992, is a Design Code VD001C converted to a Design Code OT002B timber wagon and transferred to the CCE with sleeper load. Livery is light blue/white/black with ZRA code and KRONOSPAN lettering. *Author's photo ref. W16631/DL*

Design Code VD001 40T Vanfit – Vans converted to RRA runner wagons

Certain vans were converted to RRA runner wagons with all bodywork removed. Known numbers were as follows:

RR038A (Ex-VD001A): 200659/72; 200717/27/9/34/55/82/4/95; 200828/33/52/9/74/81/94/7; 200901/5/14/6/23/7/38/43/6/9/50-2/4/61-3/72/6/8

The whole fleet of conversions appear to have been transferred to the CCE as Design Code ZE001A and given the FISHKND name BREAM.

No. DC200672, taken at Hither Green PAD on 19 March 1989, is a Design Code VD001A converted to a Design Code RR038A runner wagon and transferred to the CCE. It is in black livery with red buffer beams, ZEA code and BREAM name. *Author's photo ref. W15931/DL*

No. 200927, taken at Warrington Walton Old Junction Yard on 26 May 1984, is a Design Code VD001A converted to a Design Code RR038A runner wagon. Livery is black with RRA code. *Author's photo ref. W13917/DL*

No. DC200774, taken at Workington Yard on 16 March 1992, is a Design Code VD001A converted to a Design Code RR038A runner wagon and transferred to the CCE. It is in yellow/black livery with ZEA code and BREAM name in black. *Author's photo ref. W17163/DL*

Speedlink

No. KDC200674, taken at Goole Yard on 26 July 1992, is a Design Code VD001A van transferred to the S&T as a ZRA (Design Code ZR219A). The livery is yellow/flame red with ZRA code in white and SATLINK in black. *Author's photo ref. W17288/DL*

Design Code VD001 40T Vanfit – Vans transferred into departmental use

Certain vans were transferred into departmental use. Known numbers were as follows:

S&T: KDC200655/60/2/3/5/8/70/1/3/4/6/8-80/2/6/8/9/95/6/9; KDC200700/9/22/38/51/4/81/92/6; KDC200800/1/7/21/6/30/1/6/8/46/7/50/3/5/66/91/3/6/8/9; KDC200903/4/12/7/9/21/6/37/9/71/83/92/5-7; KDC201003/11/2/5/7/22/3/7/33/9/46/63/4/6/90; KDC210107/25/39/64/78/95/6/8, KDC210206/9/30/50/72/80/6/93; KDC210310/4/24/8/47/54/66/92

CCE: DC200890; DC200931/67/88; DC201017/72/7/8; DC210167/70; DC210215/49/79; DC210306/15/9/27/32/78

CM&E: ADC200651/2/4/6-8/61/4/6/7/9/75/7; ADC200715; ADC200815 /79; ADC210271

No. ADC210271, taken at Hoo Junction Yard on 7 December 1988, is a Design Code VD001A van transferred to the CCE as a ZRA (Design Code ZR219A). The livery is weathered flame red/grey with ZRA code in white. *Author's photo ref. W14487/DL*

No. DC200931, taken at Peterborough Yard on 3 May 1992, is a Design Code VD001A van transferred to the CCE as a ZRA (Design Code ZR219A). The livery is yellow/grey with ZRA code in white. *Author's photo ref. W16964/DL*

13
Design Code VE001
VEA 12T Van [Ammunition]

230000 to 200049 – Converted to Lot 3918 by Ashford Works, April 1978 to November 1978.

230050 to 230109 – Converted to Lot 3982 by Horwich Works, February 1981 to May 1981.

230110 to 230399 – Converted to Lot 4017 by Shildon Works, May 1982 to January 1983.

230400 to 230549 – Converted to Lot 4028 by Shildon Works, during 1983.

Design Code: VE001B; Length over headstocks: 17ft 6in; Wheelbase: 12ft 0in; Springs: Long Link; 3ft 1½in diameter wheels; Air disc brakes and hand lever; 1ft 8½in Oleo Pneumatic Buffers; Roller bearings; Instanter; TOPS Code: VEA; double-arrow/Railfreight symbol carried.

These vans were modernised Diagram 1/217 12T vacuum-braked Vanwide vans specifically to carry ammunition for the Ministry of Defence. All had roller bearings, Oleo hydraulic buffers and air brakes. The first batch, Lot 3918, was delivered in maroon livery but all later batches were delivered in flame red/grey livery. There were no modifications or transfers before 1992.

No. 230008, taken at Longhedge Junction, Battersea, in May 1978, is a Design Code VE001B VEA 12T ammunition van in brand-new condition. It is in maroon livery with white lettering, VEA code and double-arrow/Railfreight symbol. *Author's photo ref. W6885/DL*

No. 230040, taken at Hoo Junction Yard on 1 June 1989, is a Design Code VE001B 12T ammunition van. It is in flame red/grey livery with white lettering, VEA code and double-arrow/Railfreight symbol. *Author's photo ref. W16423/DL*

No. 230469, taken at Doncaster Belmont Yard on 31 May 1992, is a Design Code VE001B 12T ammunition van. It is in Sector dark grey/yellow livery with white lettering, VEA code and RfD symbol. *Author's photo ref. W17017/DL*

ABOVE No. 230238, taken at Rochester goods yard on 7 August 1984, is a Design Code VE001B 12T ammunition van. It is in flame red/grey livery with white lettering, VEA code and double-arrow/Railfreight symbol. *Author's photo ref. W14019/DL*

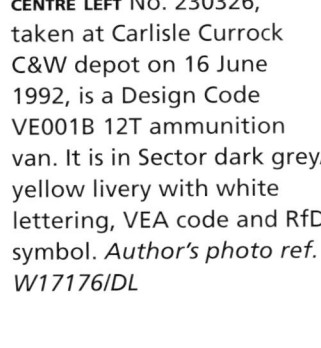

CENTRE LEFT No. 230326, taken at Carlisle Currock C&W depot on 16 June 1992, is a Design Code VE001B 12T ammunition van. It is in Sector dark grey/yellow livery with white lettering, VEA code and RfD symbol. *Author's photo ref. W17176/DL*

LEFT No. 230085, taken at Hoo Junction Yard on 22 December 1988, is a Design Code VE001B 12T ammunition van. It is in flame red/grey livery with white lettering, VEA code and double-arrow/Railfreight symbol. *Author's photo ref. W14445/DL*

No. 230286, taken at Severn Tunnel Junction Yard on 13 March 1983, is a Design Code VE001B 12T ammunition van. It is in flame red/grey livery with white lettering, VEA code and double-arrow/Railfreight symbol. *Author's photo ref. W12919/DL*

No. 230153, taken at Warrington Walton Old Junction Yard on 13 November 1983, is a Design Code VE001B 12T ammunition van. It is in flame red/grey livery with white lettering, VEA code and double-arrow/Railfreight symbol. *Author's photo ref. W13497/DL*

No. 230163, taken at Hoo Junction Yard on 22 December 1988, is a Design Code VE001B 12T ammunition van. It is in flame red/grey livery with white lettering, VEA code and double-arrow/Railfreight symbol. *Author's photo ref. W14459/DL*

No. 230548, taken at Ludgershall MoD depot on 9 March 1989, is a Design Code VE001B 12T ammunition van. It is in flame red/grey livery with white lettering, VEA code and double-arrow/Railfreight symbol. *Author's photo ref. W15493/DL*

No. 230423, taken at Southampton Bevois Park goods yard on 1 February 1989, is a Design Code VE001B 12T ammunition van. It is in flame red/grey livery with white lettering, VEAcode and double-arrow/Railfreight symbol. *Author's photo ref. W14907/DL*

The following list gives the former identities of the VEA vans:

230000 (B783814); 230001 (B784559); 230002 (B783879); 230003 (B783327); 230004 (B783722); 230005 (B782922); 230006 (B783795); 230007 (B783691); 230008 (B784016); 230009 (B784074); 230010 (B783969); 230011 (B784476); 230012 (B784352); 230013 (B783807); 230014 (B784391); 230015 (B784526); 230016 (B783790); 230017 (B784081); 230018 (B784111); 230019 (B783001); 230020 (B784304); 230021 (B782941); 230022 (B783304); 230023 (B784359); 230024 (B783219); 230025 (B783446); 230026 (B784467); 230027 (B783862); 230028 (B784833); 230029 (B784574); 230030 (B784710); 230031 (B783981); 230032 (B783810); 230033 (B783343); 230034 (B784214); 230035 (B782938); 230036 (B783876); 230037 (B783706); 230038 (B783801); 230039 (B783537); 230040 (B784828); 230041 (B783839); 230042 (B784195); 230043 (B784227); 230044 (B784335); 230045 (B784427); 230046 (B784205); 230047 (B783735); 230048 (B783277); 230049 (B784102); 230050 (B784636); 230051 (B783612); 230052 (B784072); 230053 (B783665); 230054 (B784674); 230055 (B784854); 230056 (B784810); 230057 (B784396); 230058 (B783580); 230059 (B783353); 230060 (B783668); 230061 (B783762); 230062 (B784294); 230063 (B784763); 230064 (B782874); 230065 (B783432); 230066 (B783484); 230067 (B784695); 230068 (B784375); 230069 (B783515); 230070 (B783525); 230071 (B784621); 230072 (B783713); 230073 (B784197); 230074 (B784620); 230075 (B784571); 230076 (B783766); 230077 (B784572); 230078 (B784608); 230079 (B784625); 230080 (B783227); 230081 (B783564); 230082 (B783667); 230083 (B783641); 230084 (B784638); 230085 (B784387); 230086 (B783388); 230087 (B784558); 230088 (B783239); 230089 (B783574); 230090 (B784725); 230091 (B784101); 230092 (B784265); 230093 (B783702); 230094 (B783359); 230095 (B783384); 230096 (B784739); 230097 (B784409); 230098 (B782927); 230099 (B783588); 230100 (B783678); 230101 (B783826); 230102 (B783835); 230103 (B783356); 230104 (B782948); 230105 (B782902); 230106 (B783989); 230107 (B783278); 230108 (B784157); 230109 (B784416); 230110 (B783472); 230111 (B784199); 230112 (B783571); 230113 (B784063); 230114 (B783538); 230115 (B783954); 230116 (B783075); 230117 (B784705); 230118 (B783844); 230119 (B783572); 230120 (B783126); 230121 (B784070); 230122 (B784268); 230123 (B784583); 230124 (B783006); 230125 (B783146); 230126 (B784752); 230127 (B783718); 230128 (B784392); 230129 (B783113); 230130 (B784702); 230131 (B784631); 230132 (B783745); 230133 (B784139); 230134 (B784064); 230135 (B784244); 230136 (B784699); 230137 (B783614); 230138 (B783015); 230139 (B783302); 230140 (B783213); 230141 (B784464); 230142 (B783182); 230143 (B784691); 230144 (B783877); 230145 (B783585); 230146 (B784383); 230147 (B784588); 230148 (B784772); 230149 (B783104); 230150 (B783158); 230151 (B783880); 230152 (B784511); 230153 (B784239); 230154 (B783202); 230155 (B783177); 230156 (B783417); 230157 (B784096); 230158 (B784201); 230159 (B783498); 230160 (B782907); 230161 (B783452); 230162 (B783581); 230163 (B783181); 230164 (B783407); 230165 (B783829); 230166 (B783747); 230167 (B783161); 230168 (B784759); 230169 (B783406); 230170 (B783129); 230171 (B784105); 230172 (B782882); 230173 (B783831); 230174 (B784414); 230175 (B783124); 230176 (B783950); 230177 (B783330); 230178 (B784007); 230179 (B784415); 230180 (B783119); 230181 (B784537); 230182 (B783134); 230183 (B784408); 230184 (B784421); 230185 (B784061); 230186 (B783024); 230187 (B783669); 230188 (B783609); 230189 (B783028); 230190 (B783029); 230191 (B783053); 230192 (B783118); 230193 (B783148); 230194 (B784065); 230195 (B784275); 230196 (B783030); 230197 (B783518); 230198 (B784138); 230199 (B783014); 230200 (B784539); 230201 (B784084); 230202 (B783959); 230203 (B783199); 230204 (B783873); 230205 (B783105); 230206 (B783886); 230207 (B784161); 230208 (B783049); 230209 (B784751);

230210 (B783945); 230211 (B784612); 230212 (B784337); 230213 (B784043); 230214 (B784079); 230215 (B783247); 230216 (B784273); 230217 (B783293); 230218 (B784711); 230219 (B783937); 230220 (B784364); 230221 (B783261); 230222 (B783690); 230223 (B783679); 230224 (B784551); 230225 (B783700); 230226 (B784544); 230227 (B782886); 230228 (B784162); 230229 (B783961); 230230 (B783396); 230231 (B783433); 230232 (B784495); 230233 (B783072); 230234 (Not known); 230235 (B783361); 230236 (B784384); 230237 (B784339); 230238 (B784178); 230239 (B784505); 230240 (B783140); 230241 (B783187); 230242 (B783166); 230243 (B783658); 230244 (B783748); 230245 (B783949); 230246 (B782887); 230247 (B783547); 230248 (B783502); 230249 (B784532); 230250 (B784330); 230251 (B784113); 230252 (B783929); 230253 (B783850); 230254 (B783858); 230255 (B783013); 230256 (B784371); 230257 (B783554); 230258 (B784106); 230259 (B784426); 230260 (B784011); 230261 (B783443); 230262 (B784582); 230263 (B784566); 230264 (B783891); 230265 (B784236); 230266 (B784308); 230267 (B784696); 230268 (B784243); 230269 (B783350); 230270 (B784374); 230271 (B783440); 230272 (B784619); 230273 (B783605); 230274 (B783057); 230275 (B784485); 230276 (B784747); 230277 (B784224); 230278 (B783189); 230279 (B783046); 230280 (B783422); 230281 (B783190); 230282 (B784654); 230283 (B784560); 230284 (B783902); 230285 (B783167); 230286 (B784213); 230287 (B783479); 230288 (B782942); 230289 (B783438); 230290 (B784482); 230291 (B783512); 230292 (B784299); 230293 (B783159); 230294 (B783160); 230295 (B783073); 230296 (B784744); 230297 (B783836); 230298 (B784756); 230299 (B784052); 230300 (B783557); 230301 (B782926); 230302 (B783111); 230303 (B783782); 230304 (B784649); 230305 (B782924); 230306 (B784644); 230307 (B783912); 230308 (B783286); 230309 (B783437); 230310 (B783003); 230311 (B783589); 230312 (B783321); 230313 (B784297); 230314 (B783141); 230315 (B783402); 230316 (B783198); 230317 (B783763); 230318 (B783916); 230319 (B783924); 230320 (B783577); 230321 (B784184); 230322 (B783740); 230323 (B784027); 230324 (B784740); 230325 (B783281); 230326 (B783032); 230327 (B783022); 230328 (B783090); 230329 (B783594); 230330 (B783052); 230331 (B782986); 230332 (B782952); 230333 (B784397); 230334 (B784519); 230335 (B783837); 230336 (B784211); 230337 (B784738); 230338 (B783203); 230339 (B784153); 230340 (B784173); 230341 (B783573); 230342 (B783830); 230343 (B784609); 230344 (B784279); 230345 (B782888); 230346 (B784436); 230347 (B784328); 230348 (B783559); 230349 (B784642); 230350 (B784264); 230351 (B784122); 230352 (B784502); 230353 (B783471); 230354 (B783487); 230355 (B783305); 230356 (B784550); 230357 (B784094); 230358 (B783254); 230359 (B783632); 230360 (B784394); 230361 (B783828); 230362 (B784530); 230363 (B784545); 230364 (B783120); 230365 (B784220); 230366 (B783076); 230367 (B783593); 230368 (B783798); 230369 (B784402); 230370 (B783009); 230371 (B784605); 230372 (B784437); 230373 (B783300); 230374 (B783650); 230375 (B783171); 230376 (B783208); 230377 (B784568); 230378 (B783456); 230379 (B782994); 230380 (B783270); 230381 (B783193); 230382 (B783453); 230383 (B783381); 230384 (B783492); 230385 (B783841); 230386 (B783976); 230387 (B783197); 230388 (B783395); 230389 (B783543); 230390 (B783059); 230391 (B783080); 230392 (B782912); 230393 (B783235); 230394 (B783089); 230395 (B784553); 230396 (B784185); 230397 (B783132); 230398 (B784666); 230399 (B784004); 230400 (B783136); 230401 (B784336); 230402 (B782999); 230403 (B783654); 230404 (B784499); 230405 (B784028); 230406 (B783788); 230407 (B784508); 230408 (B784707); 230409 (B782950); 230410 (B784598); 230411 (B784433); 230412 (B784514); 230413 (B784547); 230414 (B784497); 230415 (B784449); 230416 (B783131); 230417 (B784221); 230418 (B783418); 230419 (B784590); 230420 (B783165); 230421 (B783421); 230422 (B783821); 230423 (B784440); 230424 (B784470); 230425 (B784727); 230426 (B784461); 230427 (B783903); 230428 (B784058); 230429 (B784486); 230430 (B783204); 230431 (B784442); 230432 (B783180); 230433 (B783038); 230434 (B784207); 230435 (B784617); 230436 (B783996); 230437 (B783110); 230438 (B784097); 230439 (B784028); 230440 (B783366); 230441 (B784708); 230442 (B784020); 230443 (B784762); 230444 (B783010); 230445 (B784318); 230446 (B783132); 230447 (B783848); 230448 (B783130); 230449 (B784403); 230450 (B784516); 230451 (B784733); 230452 (B783125); 230453 (B784398); 230454 (B784071); 230455 (B783473); 230456 (B783077); 230457 (B783175); 230458 (B783631); 230459 (B784099); 230460 (B784298); 230461 (B784729); 230462 (B784194); 230463 (B783162); 230464 (B784632); 230465 (B784457); 230466 (B783454); 230467 (B784438); 230468 (B784606); 230469 (B782881); 230470 (B784624); 230471 (B783475); 230472 (B784579); 230473 (B784648); 230474 (B783551); 230475 (B784033); 230476 (B784086); 230477 (B783739); 230478 (B783448); 230479 (B783704); 230480 (B784570); 230481 (B783776); 230482 (B784252); 230483 (B784171); 230484 (B783393); 230485 (B784363); 230486 (B783098); 230487 (B783483); 230488 (B783834); 230489 (B784163); 230490 (B784316); 230491 (B783737); 230492 (B783888); 230493 (B783528); 230494 (B783887); 230495 (B782884); 230496 (B783196); 230497 (B784400); 230498 (B782911); 230499 (B783310); 230500 (B784077); 230501 (B782998); 230502 (B783025); 230503 (B782896); 230504 (B784245); 230505 (B783933); 230506 (B783209); 230507 (B783549); 230508 (B784561); 230509 (B784490); 230510 (B784444); 230511 (B784249); 230512 (B784344); 230513 (B783817); 230514 (B783333); 230515 (B784769); 230516 (B784500); 230517 (B784241); 230518 (B783007); 230519 (B782928); 230520 (B784059); 230521 (B784469); 230522 (B783194); 230523 (B783387); 230524 (B783142); 230525 (B783777); 230526 (B783423); 230527 (B783784); 230528 (B783064); 230529 (B784108); 230530 (B784160); 230531 (B784129); 230532 (B783510); 230533 (B783047); 230534 (B783692); 230535 (B782917); 230536 (B784735); 230537 (B784432); 230538 (B783661); 230539 (B783468); 230540 (B784418); 230541 (B783503); 230542 (B782981); 230543 (B784445); 230544 (B784032); 230545 (B783323); 230546 (B783895); 230547 (B783233); 230548 (B783282); 230549 (B783648)

14
Design Code VG001
VGA 24T Van [Sliding Wall]

210400 – Built to Lot 4007 by Shildon Works, October 1981.
210401 to 210650 – Built to Lot 4023 by Shildon Works, during 1983.
Design Code: VG001A (210400), VG001B (Remainder); Length over headstocks: 42ft 0in; Wheelbase: 29ft 5in; Springs: Brueninghaus Long Link; 3ft 1½in diameter wheels; Air clasp brakes and hand lever; 2ft 0½in Oleo Pneumatic Buffers; Roller bearings; International Screw; TOPS Code: VEA; double-arrow/Railfreight symbol carried.

The only discernible difference between 210400 and the production batch was the use of a transfer symbol on the former and nameplates, including Speedlink, on the latter. Some had gained Sector livery by the demise of Speedlink in 1991.

No. 210400, taken at Rochester goods yard in November 1981, is a Design Code VG001A VGA 24T sliding-wall van in brand-new condition. It is in unpainted/flame red/black livery with black lettering, VGA code and white double-arrow/Railfreight symbol on flame red. *Author's photo ref. W9029/DL*

ABOVE No. 210650, taken at Mossend Yard on 26 October 1988, is a Design Code VG001B sliding-wall van in original condition. It is in unpainted/flame red/black livery with white VGA code on black and no nameplates. *Author's photo ref. W14231/DL*

RIGHT No. 210495, taken at Margam Yard on 12 March 1983, is a Design Code VG001B sliding-wall van in original condition. It is in unpainted/flame red/black livery with black VGA code and double-arrow/Railfreight and Speedlink symbols in white on red plates. *Author's photo ref. W12817/DL*

RIGHT No. 210402, taken at Southampton Bevois Park goods yard on 1 February 1989, is a Design Code VG001B sliding-wall van. It is in heavily weathered unpainted/flame red/black livery with black VGA code without nameplates and with white Railfreight transfer on red. *Author's photo ref. W14941/DL*

ABOVE No. 210565, taken at Wisbech goods yard on 11 March 1984, is a Design Code VG001B sliding-wall van in original condition. It is in weathered unpainted/flame red/black livery with black VGA code and double-arrow and Speedlink symbols in white on red plates. *Author's photo ref. W13758/DL*

LEFT No. 210418, taken at Harlow Mill goods yard as part of an exhibition train on 20 February 1989, is a Design Code VG001B sliding-wall van in original condition. It is in unpainted/yellow/black livery with black VGA code and two Railfreight nameplates. *Author's photo ref. W15066/DL*

LEFT No. 210631, taken at Eastleigh Yard on 31 March 1992, is a Design Code VG001B sliding-wall van in original condition. It is in unpainted/yellow/black livery with white VGA code on black and RfD symbol. *Author's photo ref. W16628/DL*

15
Design Code XV005
XVA 80T Trestle Plate Wagon

990000 – Converted to Lot 3911 by Ashford Works, May 1977.

990001 to 990049 – Converted to Lot 3961 by Shildon Works, September 1979 to December 1970.
Design Code: XV005A; Length over headstocks: 52ft 0in; Length between bogie centres: 40ft 0in; Bogies: FBT 6 (Y25C); 3ft 1½in diameter wheels; Air block brakes on bogies and hand-wheel on bogies; 1ft 8½in Oleo Pneumatic Buffers; Roller bearings; Screw couplings; TOPS Code: XVA; No lettering carried.

These wagons were converted to different types which will be covered on the next pages.

No. 990042, taken at Scunthorpe yard in August 1980, is a Design Code XV005A XVA 80T trestle wagon in original condition. It is in flame red/black livery with white lettering and XVA code. *Author's photo ref. W8884/DL*

147

The following list gives the former identities of the XVA wagons:

990000 (B903642); 990001 (B903644); 990002 (B903613); 990003 (B903608); 990004 (B903635); 990005 (B903620); 990006 (B903645); 990007 (B903622); 990008 (B903627); 990009 (B903625); 990010 (B903633); 990011 (B903641); 990012 (B903699); 990013 (B903677); 990014 (B903623); 990015 (B903612); 990016 (B903632); 990017 (B903638); 990018 (B903690); 990019 (B903697); 990020 (B903687); 990021 (B903648); 990022 (B903626); 990023 (B903686); 990024 (B903631); 990025 (B903629); 990026 (B903679); 990027 (B903621); 990028 (B903682); 990029 (B903671); 990030 (B903607); 990031 (B903676); 990032 (B903674); 990033 (B903634); 990034 (B903684); 990035 (B903615); 990036 (B903609); 990037 (B903702); 990038 (B903692); 990039 (B903668); 990040 (B903685); 990041 (B903689); 990042 (B903683); 990043 (B903670); 990044 (B903675); 990045 (B903691); 990046 (B903700); 990047 (B903673); 990048 (B903696); 990049 (B903694)

No. 990007, taken at Scunthorpe station yard in August 1980, is a Design Code XV005A XVA 80T trestle wagon in original condition. It is in flame red/black livery with white lettering and XVA code. *Author's photo ref. W8881/DL*

All were in service on 31 July 1983 but had been converted by 21 May 1984.

By 1992; the whole fleet; with the exception of 990025; which had been withdrawn; had been converted to BOA Strip Coil wagons; as seen in the view of 990033.

No. 990024, taken at Hoo Junction Yard on 18 March 1989, is a Design Code XV005A XVA 80T trestle wagon converted to an RXA runner wagon. It is in black livery with white lettering and RXA code. *Author's photo ref. W15882/DL*

No. 990033, taken at Cardiff Tidal Sidings Yard on 6 June 1992, is a Design Code XV005A XVA 80T trestle wagon converted to a BOA coil wagon. It is in dark grey livery with white lettering, BOA code and yellow coil cradles. *Author's photo ref. W17065/DL*

No. 990016, taken at Warrington Dallam goods yard on 23 October 1988, is a Design Code XV005A XVA 80T trestle wagon converted to an RXA runner wagon. It is in black livery with white lettering and RXA code. *Author's photo ref. W14131/D*

16
Small prototype lots and air-piped conversions

960000 (ex-B922461) and 960001 (ex-B922497) – Converted to Lot 3889 by Swindon Works; January 1976; Design Code: BC008A; Length over headstocks: 45ft 0in; Length between bogie centres: 35ft 6in; Bogies: FBT 6 (Y25C); 3ft 1½in diameter wheels; Air block brakes on bogies and one hand lever; 1ft 8½in Oleo Pneumatic Buffers; Roller bearings; Instanter couplings; TOPS Code: BCA; No lettering carried.

Having commissioned a large renovations programme for the longer 42T BDO wagons; a trial was carried out on two 30T BCOs. In the event; no further examples were built; although certain BDVs with suitable bogies were given air through-pipes (see page 156 for details).

The two BCAs passed to the CM&EE; becoming YVA (Design Code YV060A).

No. 960000, taken at Scunthorpe station yard in March 1978, is a Design Code BC008A BCA 40T GLW bogie bolster wagon. It is in freight brown livery with (PROTOTYPE) BCA code. *Author's photo ref. W7309/DL*

No. 920000, taken at Stewarts Lane Depot, Battersea, in August 1979, is a Design Code BL001A BLA 58T bogie bolster wagon. It is in freight brown livery with BLA code. *Author's photo ref. W7752/DL*

920000 – Built to Lot 3896 by Ashford Works; April 1976; Design Code: BL001A; Length over headstocks and length between bogie centres: Not known; Bogies: FBT 6 (Y25C); 3ft 1½in diameter wheels; Air block brakes on bogies and hand-wheel at each end lever; 1ft 8½in Oleo Pneumatic Buffers; Roller bearings; Instanter couplings; TOPS Code: BLA; No lettering carried.

This was a lengthened version of the BBA design (see Chapter 2) but no further examples were built. This wagon passed to the CCE; being given vacuum through-pipes (as illustrated when in black livery in January 1980) and coded YNB GOLDFISH and had been scrapped by 1990.

No. DC920000 in January 1980 in black livery, having been equipped with vacuum through-pipes. *Author's photo ref. W8871/DL*

Three bogie steel designs were built in 1990; as listed below. They were not technically Speedlink wagons but have been included because they probably travelled on those services to and from works for maintenance. Numbers were:

961000 to 961003 – Built to Lot 4065 by RFS Doncaster Works; coded BGA.
962000 to 962003 – Built to Lot 4066 by RFS Doncaster Works; coded BHA.
963000 to 963003 – Built to Lot 4067 by RFS Doncaster Works; coded BJA.

No. 961001, taken at RFS Doncaster Works on 26 June 1992, is a BGA steel carrier with hood. It is in red/black livery with BGA code. *Author's photo ref. W17259/DL*

No. 962000, taken at Tees Yard on 13 June 1992, is a BHA steel carrier with hood. It is in red/black livery with BHA code. *Authors photo ref. W17110/DL*

390000 and 390001 – Built to Lot 3903 by Shildon Works; August 1976; Design Code: MF001A; Length over headstocks: 24ft 3in; Wheelbase: 15ft 0in; Springs: Long Link; 3ft 1½in diameter wheels; Air disc brakes and hand lever; 1ft 7in Oleo Pneumatic Buffers; Roller bearings; Instanter couplings; TOPS Code: MFA; No lettering carried.

These two wagons were built to carry scrap metal but seem to have been superseded by privately-owned vehicles of similar design. They were very tall wagons; as seen in the view on the next page; and perhaps this factor and the type of suspension saw them transferred into departmental use fairly quickly.

One record suggests that vacuum through-pipes may have been added at one stage but there is no evidence. Judging by the two views; taken three months apart; they do not seem to have seen much use and their ultimate fate in not known.

ABOVE No. 963003, taken at Tees Yard on 13 June 1992, is a BJA steel carrier with hood. It is in black livery with BJA code. *Author's photo ref. W17105/DL*

RIGHT No. ADC390000, taken at Basingstoke Yard on 20 March 1983, is a Design Code MF001A MFA mineral (ferrous) wagon transferred to the CM&EE. It is in weathered freight brown livery with ZRA code. *Author's photo ref. W12971/DL*

Small Prototype Lots and Air-piped Conversions – VDA 201070

It is not known if this van was used for other experiments but eventually it was converted to an OTA timber wagon which later passed to the CCE as a sleeper wagon. It retained some vestiges of the modified end seen above (see page 134).

No. 201070, taken at Mossend Yard on 17 March 1984, is a testbed van for new flexible sides. In the view below, the sides are blue with white lettering and blue VHA code. *Author's photo ref. W13802A/DL/Author's photo ref. W13802B/DL*

No. B927952, taken at Hoo Junction Yard on 1 May 1989, is a Diagram 1/484 BDV 42T bogie bolster wagon given air through-pipes and nylon securing straps. It is in rusty condition with white lettering and BDW code. *Author's photo ref. W16163/DL*

Small Prototype Lots and Air-piped Conversions – BCVs and BDVs and derivatives given air through-pipes

It was decided to upgrade two types of vacuum-fitted bogie bolster wagons to allow them to work with air-braked stock and; presumably; on Speedlink services. Both types had to be fitted with Gloucester-pattern bogies with roller bearings. In addition to the air through-pipes; as seen above; blue nylon straps for load securing were provided.

The 30T Bogie Bolster C type; Diagram 1/477; became BCW for general traffic and BTW for large pipe traffic. A few others were coded BHW and BQW but have not been recorded photographically.

The 42T Bogie Bolster D type; Diagram 1/484; became BDW for general traffic and BSW for timber traffic.

Small Prototype Lots and Air-piped Conversions – BCWs given Air through-pipes

It was planned to upgrade 425 of these vehicles; from number ranges B923100-B923299 and B924400-B924799; but there were already a number of design modifications. Vehicles known to have become BCW were as follows:

No. B924612, taken at Hoo Junction Yard on 1 July 1989, is a Diagram 1/477 BCV 30T bogie bolster wagon given air through-pipes and nylon securing straps. It is in weathered freight brown livery with white lettering and BCW code. *Author's photo ref. W16331/DL*

No. B924580, taken at Warrington Arpley Yard on 13 November 1983, is a Diagram 1/477 BCV 30T bogie bolster wagon converted to a BTV pipe wagon and given air through-pipes and nylon securing straps. It is in rusty condition with white lettering and BTW code. *Author's photo ref. W13493/DL*

B923103/4/6/7/10/1/4-6/9/23/4/7/30-2/4/7/40/2/6/55/60/9/ 71/2/4/7/83/8/9 /93/4/6-8; B923201/3/11/7/22/4/5/30/4/5/40 /7/50/1/5/66/8/9/71/3/5/8/80/2/4/6/90/2/9; B924400/6/8/11/ 2/6/8/24/32/6/7/42/3/6/7/9/50/6/62/73/8/84/6/92/8; B924503/ 6/12-5/26/7/30/44/6/61/2/4/74/8/81/6; B924604/7-10/2/8/ 23/7/30/2/7/47-9/56/7/63/9-72/4/5/80/7/93/5/9; B924704/10 /2/22/4/33/6/41/7/9/50/2/3/7/63/7 /74/5/7/82/4/93/8

Small Prototype Lots and Air-piped Conversions – BDWs given Air through-pipes

Approximately 290 BDVs; from B927800 to B928189; were upgraded to BDW from December 1982 to May 1984. Some were later converted to BSW timber wagons (see page XXX). Vehicles known to have become BDW were as follows:

B927800/3/5-10/2/4-6/8-21/4/5/7-33/5-41/4/5/7-9/53-64/6/ 7/70-2/4/6/7/9/80/2/4/6/7/9-94/6-9; B927900-3/7-16/8-20/3/ 4/6-30/2-42/4-8/51/2/5/7/9-61/3-6/8/9 /72/4-6/8/9/82/ 3/5-90/ 3/6/9; B928001/3/6/8-13/7-9/21-3/6/8-31/3-7/40-4/6/ 7/50/ 4-9/61/3/6-8/70/3-8/82-7/90/1/3-8; B928100/2-9/11/2/ 5/7/ 9-22/4-30/2-4/7/9-43/5/7/8 /50/2/3/6-9/61/2/4/5/7/70-5/7/ 9-82/4-90/3/4/8

These wagons had been converted to BTV and now became BTW. Vehicles known to have become BTW were as follows:

B923100/5/20/2/5/6/33/6/8/9/43/4/8/9/52/4/7/62/4/5/7/8/73/ 5/8/87; B923204-6/9 /14/6/8/9/26/31/7/42-4/6/8/9/54/6/62/ 3/5/72/4/7/9/94/8; B924402/4/19/21/30/3/9 /44/8/52/4/5/7/ 8/63/4/8-70/5-7/81-3/5/7/91/3/7; B924502/5/8/17/9/20/2/33 /5/7/41/5/50/1/3/6/7/63/5/8/70/3/80/5/9/90/8; B924600/1/5/ 6/15/6/20/2/34/8-40/3/4 /53/4/9/64/5/73/9/84/90/4/7; B9247 03/6/8/9/13/5/26/32/7/42/4/56/60/1/4/5/9/76/8 /81/5/94/5

No. B928104, taken at Southampton Bevois Park goods yard on 1 February 1989, is a Diagram 1/484 BDV 42T bogie bolster wagon converted to a BDW wagon and given air through-pipes and nylon securing straps. It is in rusty condition with white lettering and BTW code. *Author's photo ref. W14935/DL*

Small Prototype Lots and Air-piped Conversions – BSWs given Air through-pipes

Some BDWs were later converted to BSW timber wagons (as illustrated by B927908). Vehicles known to have become BSW were as follows:

B927887; B927908; B928031; B928132/93

No. B927908, taken at Perth goods yard on 15 June 1992, is a Diagram 1/484 BDV 42T bogie bolster wagon converted to a BSW timber wagon with tall stanchions and given air through-pipes and nylon securing straps. It is in flame red/rail grey livery with white lettering, BSW code and double-arrow/Railfreight symbol. *Author's photo ref. W17148/DL*

No. B928132, taken at Plumstead goods yard on 11 December 1988, is a Diagram 1/484 BDV 42T bogie bolster wagon converted to a BSW timber wagon with tall stanchions and given air through-pipes and nylon securing straps. It is in flame red/rail grey livery with white lettering and BSW code. *Author's photo ref. W14353/DL*

No. B927887, taken at Plumstead goods yard on 11 December 1988, is a Diagram 1/484 BDV 42T bogie bolster wagon converted to a BSW timber wagon with tall stanchions and given air through-pipes and nylon securing straps. It is in flame red/rail grey livery with white lettering and BSW code. *Author's photo ref. W14355/DL*

Conclusion

Whilst the first volume in this series examined the BR-owned wagons already available for use on Speedlink services; this volume has concentrated on those delivered during the Speedlink era.

At first brand-new designs were built but; right from the start; the fleet was augmented by refurbished older wagons. The BDA fleet were formerly unfitted and the ODA and VEA fleets were formerly vacuum-braked.

In later years; certain bogie bolster types were given air through-pipes; as detailed in Chapter 16.

Other designs were totally rebuilt for new traffic; such as the timber traffic.

The last totally new design was the VGA sliding-wall covered in Chapter 14.

In truth; BR came to prefer to be the locomotive provider for Speedlink services and increasingly preferred the customer to own; and therefore maintain; their own wagons.

European-registered wagons had always been a part of the UK scene and many new types; particularly bogie vans; appeared. Both these and UK-registered privately-owned wagons will be covered in future volumes in this series.

I have used photographs taken by me. May I conclude by thanking many like-minded enthusiasts who have helped me; in particular Paul Bartlett; Peter Fidczuk; Trevor Mann; David Monk-Steel; Andy Prime; David Ratcliffe and Roger Silsbury.

Lastly; my thanks as always go to Jean; who has helped in numerous ways to produce this book.

David Larkin
September 2024

Index

BB001 BBA Bogie Steel Wagons.................Front Cover, 15, 16, 17, 18, 19, 20, 21, 22, 23, 24, 25, 26, 27, 28, 29
BBA Bogie Steel Wagon Conversions [Ends removed & Coil cradles]........................... 30, 31
BBA Bogie Steel Wagon Conversions [BUA Hot Steel Wagon].. 31
BC008A BCA Bogie Steel Wagon............................ 150
BCW Bogie Steel Wagons [Refurbished BCV's].......... 155
BD006 BDA Bogie Steel Wagons............... 8, 32, 33, 34, 35, 36, 37, 38, 39, 40, 41, 42, 43, 44, 45, 46, 47, 48, 49, 50, 51, 52, 53, 54
BDA Bogie Steel Wagon Conversions [BFA Steel Bar Wagon]...................................... 54, 55
BDA Bogie Steel Wagon Conversions [BMA Aluminium Ingot Wagon]....................... 56, 57
BDA Bogie Steel Wagon Conversions [BTA Timber Wagon].. 58
BDW Bogie Steel Wagons [Refurbished BDV's].. 155
BGA Bogie Steel Wagons [Prototypes]... 152
BHA Bogie Steel Wagons [Prototypes]... 152
BJA Bogie Steel Wagons [Prototypes]... 153
BL001A BLA Bogie Steel Wagon 151
BP004 BPA Bogie Plate Wagons 11, 59, 60, 61, 62
BPA Bogie Plate Wagon Conversions [BMA Aluminium Ingot Wagon]............................. 63

BR006 BRA Bogie Rail Wagons........................... 10, 64, 65, 66, 67, 68
BRA Bogie Rail Wagon Conversions [YQA PARR Sleeper Wagon]...................................... 69
BSW Bogie Timber Wagons [Refurbished BDV's].. 157
BTW Bogie Pipe Wagons [Refurbished BTV's].. 156
FN003 FNA Flask Wagons [All designs]............................. 12, 70, 71, 72, 73, 74
HB001 HBA Hopper Wagons [including HEA] Rear Cover, 8, 75, 76, 77, 79, 80, 81, 82, 83, 84, 85, 86
HBA Hopper Wagon Conversions [HSA Scrap Wagon].................................. 78, 87, 88
HBA Hopper Wagon Conversions [RNA Barrier Wagon]................................. 89, 90, 91
HBA Hopper Wagon Conversions [SJA Scrap Wagon].. 92
MF001A MFA Mineral Wagons [Ferrous].................. 153
OB001A OBA Open Wagons........................Rear Cover, 7, 95, 96, 97, 98, 99, 100, 101, 102, 103, 104
OBA Open Wagon Conversions [ZCA SEA URCHIN Ballast Wagon].. 103
OBA Open Wagon Conversions [RRA Runner Wagon]... 105
OBA Open Wagon Conversions [Plasmor Block Wagon].. 106
OC001A OCA Open Wagons............................. 11, 107, 108, 109, 110

OCA Open Wagon Conversions [ZCA SEAHORSE
    Ballast Wagon].. 111, 112
OCA Open Wagon Conversions
    [OTA Timber Wagon] 112, 113, 114
OD001A ODA Open Wagons....................... 10, 115, 116
SP020A SPA Plate Wagons...........................Front Cover,
    117, 118, 119, 120, 121, 122
SPA Plate Wagon Conversions [ZCA SEAHARE
    Ballast Wagon].. 122
SPA Plate Wagon Conversions
    [SDA Double Bolster Wagon] 123
SPA Plate Wagon Conversions
    [SEA Sheeted Steel Wagon]................................. 123
SPA Plate Wagon Conversions
    [SHA Strip Coil Wagon].. 124
SPA Plate Wagon Conversions
    [SKA Wire Coil Wagon].. 124

SSA Scrap Wagons [All types]................................ 93, 94
VD001A VDA Vans ....Rear Cover,
    7, 125, 126, 127, 128, 129, 130
VDA Van Conversions
    [OTA Timber Wagon] 131, 132, 133, 134, 136
VDA Van Conversions
    [RRA Runner Wagon].. 135
VE001B VEA Vans [Ammunition]......................... 9, 137,
    138, 139, 140, 141, 142, 143
VG001A VGA Vans [Sliding-wall] 10,
    144, 145, 146
VHA Experimental Van 154
XV005 XVA Trestle Plate Wagons 9, 147, 148
XVA Trestle Plate Conversions
    [RXA Runner Wagon].................................... 148, 149
XVA Trestle Plate Conversions
    [BOA Strip Coil Wagon] 149